Business Elites

Business Elites

The Psychology of Entrepreneurs and Intrapreneurs

Reg Jennings, Charles Cox
and Cary L. Cooper

London and New York

First published 1994
by Routledge
11 New Fetter Lane, London EC4P 4EE

Simultaneously published in the USA and Canada
by Routledge
29 West 35th Street, New York, NY 10001

Typeset in Times by LaserScript, Mitcham, Surrey
Printed and bound in Great Britain by
Biddles Ltd, Guildford and King's Lynn

British Library Cataloguing in Publication Data
A catalogue record for this book is available from the British Library

ISBN 0–415–08232–3

Library of Congress Cataloging in Publication Data

Jennings, Reg.
Business elites : the psychology of entrepreneurs and intrapreneurs /
Reg Jennings, Charles Cox, and Cary L. Cooper.
    p. cm.
Includes index.
ISBN 0–415–08232–3
1. Businessmen–United States–Biography.
2. Businessmen–Psychology.
3. Entrepreneurship–Psychological aspects.
II. Cooper, Cary L.   III. Title.
HC102.5.A2J38   1994
338′.04′092273—dc20
[B]   93–48815
                                                         CIP

Contents

Figures

Tables

Acknowledgements

This work could not have taken place without the help of the entrepreneurs and intrapreneurs who participated so imaginatively, authoritatively, enthusiastically and energetically in the research, and who spent hours of their valuable time enduring our tape-recorded interviews, taking our follow-up telephone calls and answering our letters about their motivations, personality traits and background. Since the commencement of the work, some of these individuals have moved on; nevertheless, the findings remain valid.

1 Introduction

F. Scott Fitzgerald: 'The rich are different from us.'
Ernest Hemingway: 'Yes, they have more money.'

We can recognize an element of mythology in Jeffrey Archer's fictional character, the Baron Abel, in his book *Kane and Abel*. A major part of the book is devoted to preaching the gospel of enterprise and business leadership. The Baron, founder of Baron Hotels, is presented as the archetypical entrepreneur. Rising from humble beginnings as a poor Polish waiter in New York, Abel claws his way to the top of his industry, finally 'slaying', on the way up, the Boston Brahmin, Kane, who represented the establishment that was, Abel felt, responsible for much of his suffering.

Not surprisingly, these stories of the commercial success of the enterprising underdog, and the failure of the established institutions, are popular. We see the expropriators being expropriated: they catch the reader's imagination and provoke empathy, since they awaken the rebellious spirit within us. We see the entrepreneur as a bold individualist fighting the socio-economic system. He/she is that individual, who after enduring and overcoming many hardships, trials and business adventures, finally 'makes it'.

Our interest in this book, however, lies not in the mythical 'rags to riches' stories of struggling entrepreneurs, but in the 'differences and similarities' that exist between two equally important groups of real life business leaders; entrepreneurs and intrapreneurs, each of which wields considerable power, both within industry and in the world in general.

The names that spring to mind when we think of excellence in managerial intrapreneurship include many of the high street businesses and family manufacturing firms. These include the intrapreneurs who head such firms as W.H. Smith, Pilkington, Cadbury Schweppes, Geest Bananas and Schroder Wragg (the merchant bankers).

The independent entrepreneur's flair is different, and is characterized by such people as Eddy Shah, who changed the face of Fleet Street with colour newspapers; Sir Mark Weinberg and his creation, Abbey Life; Gerald Ronson who in 1966 revolutionized petrol retailing worldwide, when he introduced self-service stations; Owen Oyston with his 'No sale no fee' estate agency; Sir David Alliance who created 80,000 jobs in the last 40 years from a bankrupt textile mill in Oswaldtwistle; Teresa Gorman, MP and her scientific instruments business; and Jennifer d'Abo, chairman of Moyses Stevens Investments.

Sir Denis Thatcher, a contributor to our research, acknowledges that differences exist between entrepreneurs and intrapreneurs, and points to two main attributes: risk-taking and entrepreneurial flair, when he says,

> I am not an entrepreneur and certainly not in the class of some of your other interviewees – Shah, Bradman and Davies. As a businessman I am [still] and always have been the 'professional Director' with experience in manufacturing, marketing but mostly in finance and management information. The 'decision-maker', yes, but not with the flair of the real entrepreneur; indeed, I regard myself as cautious, *weighing* the risks more than *taking* the risks. There are *hundreds* of people like me in industry, good experienced professionals, up to date in management techniques, fairly tough and hard driving businessmen, motivated, in my case, to do the best job I can.

Ian Campbell Bradley (1987), when discussing historical entrepreneurs, isolates other 'different' distinguishing features of the entrepreneur, when he suggests that 'the entrepreneur spots and seizes opportunities which the rest of us would either miss or fail to take, whether through fear, lack of imagination or laziness'. Bradley goes on to suggest that if Titus Salt had not experimented with the contents of discarded bales he saw lying on the dockside at Liverpool in 1834, which others had written off as useless, much of the West Yorkshire worsted industry would not have been born. Similarly, if George Cadbury had not recognized the significance of the new Dutch cocoa press in 1866 and had not introduced it into Britain, his name might well have been forgotten instead of being found in every supermarket in the United Kingdom.

In another example, Bradley describes how William Lever traced the origins of his fortunes to a small decision which he took one afternoon in 1877, when he was a young commercial traveller for his father's wholesale grocery business in Lancashire. Finishing the day's calls early, he pushed on to a village outside the firm's catchment area and took half a dozen new orders. Later he pushed further and further into the area, eventually setting up a new branch which he ran himself. Five years later he set up a small soap-manufacturing firm. The firm that developed as a result of Lever deciding to do more, instead of less, work one afternoon is now the largest producer of consumer goods in the world, Unilever.

These stories are not uncommon examples of entrepreneurship, and are excellent biographical accounts of how some leading figures started and developed their businesses. We can infer that these actions are not the actions of ordinary men and women. It is in the attempt to better understand these extraordinary people that we have been collecting data aimed at defining some of the personal characteristics of successful individuals. Rather than knowing how they started, our focus is on finding out something about what they are really like. We have been fortunate enough to obtain the cooperation of people of equal stature to Bradley's historical entrepreneurs, who have given their time to contribute to this study.

ENTREPRENEURIAL AND INTRAPRENEURIAL TYPES

There is a difference between the chief executive of W.H. Smith Ltd, Cadbury Schweppes PLC or Pilkington PLC, who have risen to their positions in their companies by progress through the corporate hierarchy, and individuals like Sir David Alliance, Gerald Ronson, Owen Oyston, Sir Mark Weinberg, Godfrey Bradman or Eddy Shah, who started from the bottom and now control their own multimillion-pound firms. The executives of W.H. Smith's, Cadbury's and Pilkington's we call 'elite intrapreneurs'. The latter group are referred to as 'elite independent entrepreneurs'. The term intrapreneur is derived from an article by Macrae (1976), writing in *The Economist*, about the 'coming entrepreneurial revolution'. The idea was developed and popularized by Pinchot (1985). By intrapreneur, Pinchot meant an individual who operated in an entrepreneurial way, but from within an established organization. This was to distinguish this individual from the 'entrepreneur', who built up his or her own business. The intrapreneur can operate at any level in the business. He/she does not have to be a chief executive. We have borrowed the term, and used it here to refer to our highly successful executives, to distinguish them from the entrepreneurs, and because they are also intrapreneurs in the sense in which Pinchot uses the term.

The term entrepreneur was first coined in the eighteenth century by Richard Cantillon, who identified the risk-bearing function of an entrepreneur. The term elite independent entrepreneur, which we propose to use, came into prominence later and was used by Bruce (1976) to differentiate different types of entrepreneurs: model, independent and ubiquitous. By elite we mean those people who have reached the top in their chosen field and have become multi-millionaires. They are the people who 'have' the most of whatever is available of any given value or set of values (Mills, 1956), or, as Pareto (1963) describes the term:

> Let us assume that in every branch of human activity each individual is given an index which stands as a sign of his capacity, very much the same way as the way in which grades are given in examinations at schools. The highest type of lawyer, for instance, will be given 10. The man who does not get a client will be given 1 – reserving zero for the man who is an out and out idiot. To the man who has made his millions – honestly or dishonestly as the case may be – we will give 10. . . . so let us make a class for people who have the highest indices in their branch of activity and to that class give the name of elite.
>
> (Pareto, 1963)

Figure 1.1 defines and shows the relationship between the various categories of intrapreneurs and entrepreneurs, elite and ubiquitous.

Elite independent entrepreneurs

These are individuals who have started their own companies, building them into very large corporations, in which they still have or had a very large holding. They are usually major shareholders, and hold or held a controlling interest. They are all multi-millionaires and include high-profile

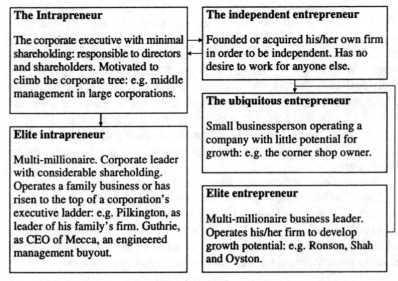

Figure 1.1 Entrepreneurial and intrapreneurial types

people in the international business world. The individuals we interviewed included:

SIR DAVID ALLIANCE, who came to England as a 17-year-old Iranian immigrant, started in textiles and now operates one of the biggest groups in Europe employing over 80,000 people.

LORD ARCHER, millionaire bestselling author, recovering from catastrophic financial failure.

TONY BERRY, former chairman of Blue Arrow PLC, the largest employment agency in the world.

GODFREY BRADMAN, property developer.

SIR NIGEL BROACKES, chairman, Trafalgar House.

DAME CATHERINE COOKSON, DBE, DLitt, MA, author.

JENNIFER d'ABO, chairman of Moyses Stevens Investments Ltd.

GEORGE DAVIES, creator of NEXT, the high street chain of fashion stores.

PETER de SAVARY, financier, one time owner of the northernmost and southernmost tips of Great Britain.

ROBERT GAVRON, chairman, St Ives Printing (now semi-retired).

TERESA GORMAN, MP, former innovator and entrepreneur.

PETER GUMMER, founder of the largest PR firm in the world.

TOM HUGHES, hotelier.

VICTOR KIAM II, president of the Remington Corporation.

CHRIS NICHOLSON, chairman of the Easdale Island Shipping Line Ltd, also former owner and Laird of Easdale Island.

OWEN OYSTON, chairman and CEO, The Oyston Group of Companies.

GERALD RONSON, financier, founder of the self-service petrol stations.

EDDY SHAH, who changed the method of newspaper printing in the UK.

SIR MARK WEINBERG, founder of Abbey Life.

HAROLD WOOLF, executive chairman, Underwood (Chemists) Ltd.

LORD YOUNG, former entrepreneur and the minister who helped set the parameters for the Enterprise Society in Britain.

Note: Some entrepreneurs who agreed to be interviewed wished to remain anonymous. We have respected this, and have not included their names, only quotations, in the book.

Elite intrapreneurs

Members of this group have generally risen to their positions as chief executives by working up through the corporate structure of major and highly successful companies. While they are instrumental to the development and expansion of the organization, they did not contribute to its foundation. Essentially they are employees of the organization. In this group, many were members of the original founding family, and all are multi-millionaires. They were:

FRANCIS BAILEY, president, Bailey's Retail.
SIR NORMAN BURROUGH, CBE, former chairman Beefeater Gin.
SIR ADRIAN CADBURY, recently retired chairman Cadbury Schweppes.
MICHAEL GUTHRIE, former chairman, Mecca PLC, currently CEO of Bright Reasons, PLC.
DAVID JONES, chairman, NEXT PLC.
SIR KENNETH KLEINWORT, banking.
MARTIN LAING, CBE, chairman John Laing PLC, civil engineering.
The late LORD McALPINE of Moffat, civil engineering.
EMMA NICHOLSON, MP, computer software expert.
JOHN H. PATTISSON, former director, Hanson PLC.
SIR ANTONY PILKINGTON, chairman, Pilkington.
DANIEL ROSE, president, Rose Associates Inc., New York.
NIGEL RUDD, chairman, Williams Holdings PLC.
BARON BRUNO SCHRODER, director, J. Henry Schroder Wagg PLC.
JULIAN SMITH, former director, W.H. Smith Ltd.
SIR DENIS THATCHER, finance and management.
LEONARD van GEEST, former chairman, Geest PLC.
SAM WHITBREAD, former chairman, Whitbread & Co. Ltd.

Note: Some intrapreneurs who were interviewed wished to remain anonymous. They will be quoted, but not mentioned by name.

The two groups – elite independent entrepreneurs and elite intrapreneurs – provide a comparison between those who start companies and those who help maintain and develop them. In this book we will discuss some of the major similarities and differences we have found between the two groups.

WHAT INFORMATION DID WE REQUIRE?

Both groups took part in semi-structured interviews and answered questionnaires, from which we were able to collate information on the following aspects of their lives:

CHILDHOOD – including parental influence, separation, and deprivation in childhood.
SOCIAL ORIGINS – to investigate effects of different socio-economic backgrounds on each group, including marginalization, social status and stratification.

EDUCATION – to see if anything was distinctive about each group's educational background.

'GUARDIAN ANGELS' – what help or support from family, friends or mentors did each group receive?

APPROACH TO WORK – what managerial styles do they exhibit and how do they relate to others?

THE WORK ETHIC – what codes, values and ethics does each group follow?

PERSONALITY – what traits or characteristics distinguish the two groups from each other and from the rest of ordinary workers/employees?

CHARITY/PHILANTHROPY – the individuals who form the subjects of this study are noted for their charitable contributions. We are interested in the motivations behind their actions.

STRUCTURE OF THE RESEARCH

Sonnenfelt and Kotter (1982) outline four major phases in the maturation of career theory:

The personality trait approach: These theories, developed in the 1920s, looked at the relationship between personality and vocational choice. This approach depicted a static individual in a static world, which may have been a reflection of the stability of the period.

The social structure approach: This approach began in the 1930s. It attempted to identify determinants of occupational attainment external to the individual, such as social class.

The career stage approach: The 1950s saw a freeing up of society and a more dynamic approach to career theories was adopted. This acknowledged that an individual's career changes, and that different stages are marked by different needs, concerns, commitments, aspirations and interests.

Life cycle theories: The notion of developing one's career over an entire lifetime is relatively recent (Hall, 1976). In this approach adulthood is no longer viewed as a static period, but as a period of change and development. Hall, for example, defined career as: 'an individually perceived sequence of attitudes and behaviours associated with work related experiences and activities over the span of a *period of a person's life*'.

The research by Sonnenfelt and Kotter in the 1970s on life cycle theory provided a richer more dynamic view of career stages, which recognized that careers reflect and interact with the individual's life – past, present and future. Borrowing, modifying and applying the idea of Sonnenfelt and Kotter's (1982) Model of Career Development allowed us to trace the occupational structure of both groups of business leaders. This modified Sonnenfelt and Kotter model, used by us as a conceptual model for determining and organizing the information collected during the interviews from both groups of business leaders, is outlined in Figure 1.2.

AUDIENCE EFFECT

As indicated earlier, this study is based on self-reports: in effect, on how entrepreneurs and intrapreneurs see themselves. Consequently, we were very aware of potential 'audience problems'. What is meant by 'audience problems' in field research is outlined by Becker (1958). He suggests that one of the major considerations involved in the analysis of interview data is that, whatever its form, it is not to be taken at face value, as unproblematically representing the world it is supposed to describe. Only by investigating the processes by which it was generated can we determine its implications and decide what inferences can legitimately be drawn from it.

So a primary consideration in analysing data from an interview is the audience to which the accounts reported were directed. They will be shaped to one degree or another by the respondents' expectations regarding who might hear what they are disclosing. Furthermore, respondents with significant powers, such as elite entrepreneurs and intrapreneurs, will disclose information with particular types of audience in mind. These considerations will shape the nature of the interview, by determining what is taken to be relevant, what can be assumed to be existing knowledge, what should not be said and what must be said to maintain the image. We recognize the possibility that what we are tapping may be highly developed and sophisticated rationales. For example, how should the answers to questions on philanthropy, charity, honesty and the work ethic be treated? Do these answers genuinely reflect the reasons underlying the behaviour?

Following Becker's (1958) recommendations, we should distinguish in the analysis between statements which are direct responses to the questions and those that are volunteered. We must remember that even 'spontaneous' utterances may be shaped to certain concepts of the interviewer. The informant may suspect that the interviewer may not be the only perceived audience, and will be aware that the interviewer is passing on what the informant has said to others, either anonymously or by attributed quotation. To overcome these problems we have, where possible, tried to verify the statements made by the interviewees/respondents with a 'third party'. We have also in most cases checked and cross-checked interview material with the respondents themselves.

	EDUCATION		**WORK HISTORY**
WORK SPACE	Amount of education Type of education		'Guardian angel'/mentor Family influence Job to job – spiral career path Work up through corporate structure – linear career path
	THE INDIVIDUAL'S PERSONALITY		**ADULT DEVELOPMENT HISTORY**

PERSONAL SPACE	Core traits
	Motivations: wealth, power, need
	   to achieve, independence
	Adaptor/innovator
	Ability as a verbal communicator
			Changes in priorities, due to financial failure
			Management style: baron, visionary, coach,
			   traditionalist
			Goals: means oriented/ends oriented
			Risky/risk-averse

	CHILDHOOD/FAMILY ENVIRONMENT		
NON-WORK/ FAMILY SPACE	Father's occupation Social background Relationship with parents Loss of a parent Shaping events		

PAST ———————— CHILDHOOD ———— ADULTHOOD ———————— FUTURE

ENTREPRENEUR
or
INTRAPRENEUR

Figure 1.2 The structure of this research

Modified from Sonnenfelt and Kotter's (1982) Career Development Model

THE ORGANIZATION OF THIS BOOK

Although the research on which this book is based, was designed using the model by Sonnenfelt and Kotter (1982), for the sake of greater clarity and ease of conceptualization the following chapters are arranged in, more or less, chronological order: we start from childhood, work through education to adult development and personality. However, before starting on this sequence we provide, in the next chapter, an outline of the careers of a number of entrepreneurs and intrapreneurs as a sample of the type of data with which we are dealing. This also gives a very good feel of the lives and characteristics of the people this book is about. We conclude this chapter by drawing out a few of the issues with which we are concerned.

In Chapter 3 we start the chronological sequence by analysing the early background of our subjects and tracing the effect, on their lives, of childhood events. This leads us (in Chapter 4) to an analysis of subjects' socio-economic background, and we look at the effects of marginalization, particularly its influence on the development of entrepreneurs. In Chapter 5 we examine the influence of education, including the effect of mentors or 'guardian angels', a term used by one of our interviewees. From education, we move (in Chapter 6) to the world of work, looking especially at concepts of the 'work ethic' and its influence on the development of entrepreneurship. A fairly detailed analysis of the personalities of both the intrapreneur and the entrepreneur is given in Chapter 7. This includes consideration of creativity, approach to risk, motivation and managerial style.

Most of the top business leaders who form the subject of this book are noted for their philanthropy and charitable work. This seemed to be an important aspect of their lives, and so in Chapter 8 we examine their approach to this activity and what appear to be motives underlying it. In Chapter 9 we provide an overview of the background and characteristics of the elite business leader, and in the final chapter, we offer a few reflections on the future of entrepreneurship in the 1990s.

EXECUTIVE SUMMARY

This book is about elite entrepreneurs and intrapreneurs. By 'elite' we mean highly successful. They are all heading very large and successful organizations. They are all successful in the sense that they are wealthy, being multi-millionaires. By entrepreneurs, we mean individuals who have started their own businesses and built them into large organizations. The intrapreneurs are individuals who are heading large corporations of which they are not the owner and which they did not themselves develop. They may, however, be a major or minor shareholder, although they are members of the family of the original founder. We were interested in what motivates these individuals and what factors contribute to their development.

The study was based on in-depth interviews and questionnaires. We set out to investigate the influence of such factors as childhood experience, socio-economic background, education, approach to work, personality and philanthropic activity. The study is based on a model which suggests that the individual's career is determined by a complex interaction of these factors.

2   Elite business careers

We were interested in the life histories of both intrapreneurs and entrepreneurs because we wanted to discover what similarities and
differences accounted for the varying methods of achieving leadership
and success in large organizations. We began by analysing the case
histories of some prominent business leaders in both groups and found
that entrepreneurs in particular could isolate significant events and
experiences in their lives that they believed shaped their future career
and their success.

As an example, our study found that entrepreneurs had appreciably
more 'significant happenings' in forming their career paths than intrapreneurs. Entrepreneurs nearly all spoke of occasions when they were
faced with challenges that required them to cope without outside
support.

The following career histories illustrate the importance of significant
life and career events on the development of business leaders, and give
some prototypic examples of the type of data generated by this research.

CASE HISTORIES – ENTREPRENEURS

Sir David Alliance

Sir David Alliance was born in Iran, the son of a Jewish merchant. He
started work at the age of 13, continuing his studies in the evening, and
started his own textile business three years later. He came to Britain in
1950, aged 17, searching out suppliers, but decided to stay and join the
British textile industry. During our interview, Sir David talked about the
uncertainty he felt in coming to England, the effort required to set up his
business, and the influences and role models which affected his
entrepreneurial career path.

Leaving behind the country of your birth and moving to a new country is a great challenge. Adapting to a new way of life, local customs, etc. requires a great deal of creativity to get on. It was this creativity that has helped me deal with the many hurdles I have had to overcome in business over the years. . . . .

Fortunately or unfortunately business has always been my life. I started working and studying at the age of 13. Admittedly this did not leave me much time for anything else. I came to this country at the age of 17 to buy goods for Iran and slowly but surely picked up the business. The first company I bought was a weaving mill in Oswaldtwistle which was on the point of receivership. I paid off all the creditors in full, and within a very short time the company was making a profit.

We asked Sir David about his fears and expectations when he took charge of his first bankrupt mill.

Of course, I was concerned, but I was not afraid. My main concern was the very high rate of interest at which I borrowed the money. I borrowed the money at 28 per cent. In fact it worked out at 34 per cent with a bank rate of 4.5 at the time. It might come as a surprise but I borrowed the money from a car dealer.

Sir David then went on to talk about the talents one needs if one is to survive as an entrepreneur.

First you have to know yourself. You have to be very honest with yourself and know your limitations. You have to set yourself objectives but you have to be realistic. Then, by putting your heart and soul into it you will achieve those objectives. Of course there will be many obstacles along the way, but by using your creativity, and provided you have enough determination, you will find a way round them.

Business is complex; you need to have more than one talent. You have to be a good all-rounder. However, I believe the single most important talent you need is the ability to choose the right team.

Remember, you cannot have two masters. You have to choose the business or yourself. You have to forget about yourself. And forget money. In my working life money has never been my goal. My primary focus has always been to produce the right goods at the right time. Profit is the by-product – a kind of measure of your success, of how well you are doing.

When asked about role models or shaping events in his life, he explained that he had not followed in his father's footsteps.

Not in a direct sense, but family approval has always been very important to me. I always think to myself, how would they view what I am doing?

In terms of specific shaping events which had helped his career develop along entrepreneurial lines, Sir David said:

I think it has a lot to do with the way I was brought up – my home environment. My father always talked to us about his day at the office. When I got my first job, which was as the office boy to a wholesaler, I felt immediately at home. I was totally committed from the start. I felt it was my business and not somebody else's. This sense of ownership made me think, if this was my business, how would I run it? This first step up the career ladder and the lessons learnt have been invaluable over the years.

Later we discussed if it was possible to teach special entrepreneurial skills to young people.

I do not believe entrepreneurial skills can be taught in the conventional sense. They have more to do with the way you are brought up and the influences around you from a very early age. Entrepreneurs in the main, but not always, have lived in a work environment with parents who have talked to them about their work. It is, of course, important to remember that not all entrepreneurs are involved in building a business and making money. They can be found in many different walks of life. The thing that distinguishes them as entrepreneurs is their self-motivation, their desire to accept a challenge and the contribution they make. The entrepreneurs I have greatest admiration for are those who contribute to society.

When asked what advice he had for potential entrepreneurs, Sir David replied:

I am always delighted to talk to potential entrepreneurs and give them guidance. However, it is important to remember that no two people operate in the same way. I can offer advice, but the individual must then adopt his own approach. The best advice I can give is to put your heart and soul into it and not to allow yourself to be deterred by any mistakes you make along the way. Whatever you are doing, always strive to find a better way of doing it and make sure you use your creative talents to best advantage.

Sir David's skills have kept him at the top into the 1990s. Briefly, he bought his first textile mill in Oswaldtwistle in 1953 for £8,000. In 1964 he bought J.D. Williams, a mail-order company that specialized in inexpensive clothing. This is now a family controlled business, called N. Brown

Investments, and it turned over £200 million in 1988. Sir David owns 50 per cent of the shares, and his brother Nigel owns 25 per cent. N. Brown reported a 21 per cent rise in pre-tax profits in the six months to the end of September 1993.

In the 1970s when the British textile industry was in accelerated decline, Sir David bought Spirella, a company making women's foundation garments. He steered the company into profit and then merged with Vantona, one of the biggest names in textiles. Today Sir David is chairman of Coats Viyella, one of Europe's largest textile groups. According to *Money* magazine (1988), it is the jewel in the Alliance crown. In 1982, he took over Carrington Viyella, raising its annual profit from £12 million to £21 million. Later he merged with Nottingham Manufacturing, a company supplying Marks & Spencer with knitwear and hosiery. In February 1986 the group purchased Coats Patons for £708 million.

Although Sir David was a victim of the 1987 stock market crash, which saw his shareholdings plunge by £73 million, he has since recovered, and he is weathering the effects of recession. In 1991 Coats Viyella acquired the Tootal textile group, in which it had previously held a 29 per cent interest. Sir David's organization has plants in 60 countries, a workforce of 80,000 and produces some of the top brands, including Ladybird, Van Heusen and Jaeger. Group pre-tax profits in 1992 were £109 million, and in the first half of 1993 were £62.8 million, up 35 per cent on the previous year. Twice married, Sir David was knighted by Margaret Thatcher for his contribution to her concept of enterprise culture. Sir David has homes in London and Manchester. He enjoys collecting objets d'art and has a passion for Lowry.

Peter de Savary

Like Sir David Alliance, Peter de Savary's career path was far from easy. It reflects de Savary's lack of formal education and his need to 'find himself' by emigrating. It also highlights the entrepreneur's ability to grasp and develop opportunities others cannot or will not see.

In a slightly light-hearted way, we were interested to know why Peter de Savary employs such a high proportion of extremely beautiful, elegantly dressed women on his staff. Why, one had to ask, would de Savary, a businessman, expose himself to sniping media criticism about sexism, if the only benefit was simply to be surrounded by beautiful women? Is it by design, or was it a chance event? The answer was refreshingly simple – de Savary employs women because he feels that they are more competent and more loyal than men.

I think that one of the things about going to work is that you must keep your sense of humour throughout the day. Drab, boring businessmen don't enhance that feeling; attractive women do. Secondly, in my experience, wherever you can get a woman to do a job, wherever she has the skills and the dedication – because so many more women are dedicated to their husbands and their children or whatever – but where you can get dedicated businesswomen, I find their level of conscientiousness is higher, their tidiness and good housekeeping and their work; and how they proceed about their business is much neater and together than the average man. More important than anything is their loyalty. I've always employed a high proportion of women and I give them a lot of responsibility. The lady that you have just been listening to on the intercom is the main board director of a very large public company.

De Savary was asked what keeps him on top in his work:

I don't fantasize or imagine, then leave it alone. I find that very frustrating. I would rather put it out of my mind if I can't do it. . . . Most of what I do is creative, and very little hi-tech or financially sophisticated. I basically take something that most people regard as they see it, but in my eyes it's a catalyst for a creation of some type. So I normally take a troublesome situation, or an unwanted real estate, or a troubled business, and try to inject into them a new level of creativity that totally transforms them into something very different. I'm very much a pioneer, inasmuch as I don't buy success, I buy problems.

Regardless of de Savary's flamboyant attitude, he still nurses the fear that most entrepreneurs have: fear of catastrophic failure:

I fear it absolutely. It is that fear that keeps you on your toes. That's the real difference: I have to make decisions, and take and make commitments – not necessarily financial, but human, emotional, moral, financial, of every type. The vast majority of people never have to go to bed at night and wake up in the morning with those commitments on their backs of such a magnitude that it's enormous, and upon which perhaps thousands of other people's jobs, livelihoods and success depends, and that is a big responsibility.

We asked about role models or possible shaping events in his work career, but de Savary didn't feel that he could select any one person or happening.

No, not really. No, not in an individual sense . . . I think that I've always had a desire . . . and have felt that in today's world there is a lacking of the true sense and spirit of adventure and pioneering that probably existed in the last century. To that degree, I try to repeat that kind of feeling in my life today. Ideally, I would have liked to have lived 150 years ago, when there was perhaps a high degree of romance and a higher degree of real pioneering and adventure than exists today. Today's communications and transportation have taken away much of the intrigue, the romance, the adventure and the mystique for the entrepreneur. So I try to put into my life what I think would have been there 150 years ago. If you like, that's my model . . . it's not a person.'

When asked what advice he had for potential entrepreneurs, de Savary replied:

I would tell him or her two things. OK I know you could tell them a hundred things, but I would tell them two. Always remember to treat all classes of people the same way. Be nice to the important people and be just as nice to the little people and those in between. So whether you are dealing with the Chairman of a big bank, which is very important to you, or whether you are dealing with a doorman at the restaurant, treat them the same. Secondly, always remember to leave a good squeeze in the lemon for the next man; that means, never over-negotiate, never be too greedy. A profit is a profit and the man that tries to squeeze a bit more usually ends up an unhappy man. Now, we all know we can get more juice out of the lemon, but it doesn't give you any more satisfaction.

Peter de Savary is a keen yachtsman who has tried twice for the America's Cup. He was born in Essex, the son of a furniture maker, and attended Charterhouse School, where he achieved an O level in religious instruction. At 16 he left England for Canada where he worked as a duplicator salesman and later developed a babysitting business. It occurred to him that people needed gardening and house-cleaning services, so he developed a three-tier business centred on the home. Observing the obvious and providing services that people needed was to become the hallmark of de Savary's entrepreneurial style. He returned from Canada at the age of 21, and joined his father's business. After three years as production manager, he asked his father for a rise (to £3,000 a year), but was refused. He left the family business for 'a world-wide odyssey', and set off again to sow the seeds of his business empire around the world. His travels took him to Africa, South America and the Middle East.

In Nigeria he saw the opportunities for trading in oil and cement, and established a very successful business. In 1977 he became a director of a Kuwait- and London-based bank. His interests range from oil to property. His homes include Littlecote House in Wiltshire, a flat in London and bases in New York and the Caribbean. In October 1987 de Savary made

£22 million by selling his St James's Clubs in London and Paris. He bought Land's End, Cornwall, in 1987, but has since resold it.

Lord Young

Lord Young, another 'high flyer' in the entrepreneurial world of the 1970s and 1980s, recalls his developmental history:

> I was born in 1932, my father was first generation immigrant. He came over from Lithuania in 1905, aged five. My mother's parents lived in this country already; I think they were second generation. I was born in Stamford Hill, I grew up in East London, well, the east side of London. I went to school during the war and after the war. I left school at 16 to become an articled clerk ... I've made much of the fact that I left school at 16, but it was the traditional way to become a solicitor. I was going to become a film director, I was going to be an apprentice, but the British film industry went into one of its crises so I became articled to an uncle who was a solicitor.
>
> I did five years' articles and in the middle of that I decided to take a degree at University College, which I did as an evening student. I had started playing golf as a young man and ended up playing golf for the university. I qualified as a solicitor, practised for less than a year and joined Great Universal Stores [GUS]. That was a blinding flash – a revelation. Because I suddenly realized that life was about 'can-do', whereas before it was about 'can't-do', or advising people not to. Within about eighteen months, I started to work for Isaac Wolfson. I worked for him – my first cousin had married his son, his only son. He heard me speak at the wedding and because of that he offered me a job, and I decided that I wouldn't turn down the chance. I worked for him for five years then I realized that I wanted to go on my own.
>
> I left in 1961, when I was 29 to set up my own business, which I did in real estate property. I was building industrial estates. I managed to borrow the money and get going. I started off sharing half in a small office with my brother, who was just a newly qualified accountant, who ended up chairman of the BBC, he died two years ago. My parents gave us the best of everything: a good education and no money! So that left us with incentives. Stewart carried on as an accountant and, as I've said, I qualified as a lawyer: five years with GUS, then I went to start up my own business in 1961, and continued to build up a reasonable-sized group called Eldonwall.
>
> By the 1970s I had sold out to Town & City. I stayed there for two or three years, but got fed up with that. . . . I set up something new with

Manufacturers Hanover, which prospered, and in a few years I had got myself back on my feet. Then I got terribly fed up with the Labour Party. I had voted Labour until 1964, but got disillusioned with Harold Wilson and wouldn't touch Labour after 1966, but I never voted Tory. I thought Ted Heath was the answer to a maiden's prayer but got fed up after he made his 'U'-turn. I knew that corporatism was not for me. The irony is that I became a member of one of those great corporatist bodies in later days. But anyway, in 1975 after I had thought about emigrating and I had decided not to, I went to work for Keith Joseph and sold out my business interest in March of 1979.

Tony Berry

Perhaps for Tony Berry, the former chairman of Blue Arrow Ltd, the climb to the top was a little easier. Like many of his peers, he has always been a high achiever. The most important thing for him at school was sport, and he displayed great talent, not only in football and cricket (he played as a junior for Spurs and Middlesex), but also in boxing where he was Junior ABA Schoolboy Boxing Champion (1957). His parents always encouraged him to 'get on'. Any hopes of 'making it' in any of these sporting fields were effectively dashed when he damaged a ligament during a football match while playing for top amateur club Barnet.

Born on 22 October 1940, Tony Berry attended Latymer School, Edmonton, north London, where he achieved passes in nine O levels and two A levels. He is the son of an electrician and comes from a working-class background, 'the Coronation Street of Edmonton'. His elite entrepreneurial status has been achieved without the benefit of a public school education or the 'right contacts' culled from the right university. He became a management trainee with Guinness and it was here that he thought he needed to get 'qualified' in something and took the examinations of the Association of Certified Accountants.

After ten years at Guinness, Berry was approached for a job as chief accountant by the financial director of Bovril, whose secretary just happened to be Berry's first wife. It really was a bit of a set-up:

> as ever it's not what you know, it's who you know . . . I certainly wasn't qualified for the job, for which they paid me an exorbitant salary.

The 18 months he spent at Bovril were invaluable to Berry:

> You do swim, you know. It's amazing what you can do when you're thrown in at the deep end. It concentrates the mind.

He decided to accept an offer made to him at a cricket match by his friend, David Evans, chairman of management services company Brengreen Holdings, to join the company as corporate development and financial controller: 'So I left a very secure job at Bovril with sophisticated systems and beautiful plush offices to go and sit over a drain in Shoreditch.'

Berry built up the company from a turnover of £200,000 in 1969 to £23 million by December 1981. But after 12 years, in December 1981, he was sacked and to this day does not know why: 'It was the biggest shock of my life. If I'd pinched £100,000 from the till, I could have understood it. I couldn't believe it.'

With a £150,000 golden handshake, and a further £350,000 raised by selling his Brengreen shares, he opened a consultancy and came into contact with Sheila Watson-Challis, who wanted help running her small staff recruitment agency and holiday tour company, Blue Arrow. Berry took his first entrepreneurial step when he took control of Blue Arrow on 1 July 1982: a company with losses of £300,000 in six months. He boosted the company into profit: within one year he had turned the loss into a £211,000 profit. He bought a 55 per cent stake in Blue Arrow for £350,000 cash and £700,000 in convertible loan notes and within three years had launched it on the unlisted securities market with a value of £3.1 million. By 1985 the company was worth £85 million and was the largest staff recruitment and contract cleaning firm in Britain. By the beginning of 1987 following a series of acquisitions, most notably Brook Street Bureau and Hoggett Bowers in the UK and Tempories Inc. and Positions Inc. in America, the company had a stock market valuation of £350 million and profits of £20 million. In August 1987, Berry successfully launched a bid of £767 million for the US employment agency, Manpower, funded by a £837 million rights issue, the largest successful rights issue in British financial history at the time. With this acquisition, Blue Arrow became the world's largest employment services group.

Berry helped co-sponsor the 1989 British America's Cup challenge with Peter de Savary, putting in £8.5 million. He has a 10 per cent stake in Tottenham Hotspur – a team he once played for as a junior. He is currently deputy chairman of Tottenham Hotspur PLC and chairman of Business Technology Group PLC, a listed public company specializing in copier and office machines. He is also chairman of Profit Builder PLC.

Sir Mark Weinberg

Abbey Life Assurance Company, and Hambro Life Assurance (now called Allied Dunbar Assurance) are names that conjure up images of the very bedrock on which Britain's financial institutions are built, suggesting the solid building blocks of the enterprise society. They are almost synonymous with the Refuge, the Pearl . . . even the Bank of England. It is as though there was never a time when they did not exist – they have a degree of permanence – but to think this would be wrong. Abbey Life was started in 1961; Hambro Life ten years later. They were created by Mark Weinberg, a young immigrant, who arrived in England both penniless and friendless: 'I didn't have any money, I didn't know anybody.'

Mark Weinberg, the son of a South African insurance salesman, was born in South Africa in 1931. He received a Bachelor of Commerce and Bachelor of Laws at the University of the Witwatersrand. Later he received his Master of Laws at the London School of Economics, specializing in company law. He practised at the Johannesburg Bar before settling in England. On arrival in London, he found investors to put up £50,000 and founded Abbey Life Assurance Company – one of the first companies to introduce unit-linked assurance policies. In 1971, with the backing of Hambros Bank, he headed the team that founded Hambro Life Assurance, which is the largest unit-linked assurance company in the UK.

Weinberg resigned as chairman of Allied Dunbar in October 1990, and is executive chairman of St James's Place Capital PLC, the parent company of the J. Rothschild Group. He has participated in the formation of yet another life assurance company, J. Rothschild Assurance. Until July 1990 he was deputy chairman of the Securities and Investment Board (SIB), the practitioner-based regulatory authority for the investment and life assurance markets.

He is the author of the standard textbook *Weinberg & Blank on Takeovers and Mergers*, now in its fifth edition. Sir Mark is chairman of the Financial Development Board of the NSPCC and co-chairman of the Per Cent Club, a group of top companies committed to increasing companies' charitable and community contributions. He was also a trustee of the Tate Gallery and is chairman of Judging of the Prince of Wales Award for Innovation and Production. He founded and provides the funding for the Foundation for Communication for the disabled. Sir Mark is married to actress Anouska Hempel, who is an entrepreneur in her own right with Blake's Hotel and a couture dress designing business.

Sir Mark can be seen as exploiting the advantages attributable to 'stranger value' when he says:

> I have often said that I had a great advantage coming into the City of London with a South African accent. Because if I had come with an English accent from the wrong side of the tracks then I would have been unacceptable in the City.

But having an acceptable accent or not, the City is unforgiving if you fail, so together with the correct accent he must have an idea that worked. By analysing the interview, we may understand more fully Sir Mark's career path. Sir Mark Weinberg is perhaps the most highly educated of all the entrepreneur group, and is still one of Britain's leading entrepreneurs – although he feels that his later ventures were less entrepreneurial.

Describing his work history, Sir Mark talked about the different characteristics of entrepreneurs and non-entrepreneurs.

> Certainly, I would think that the characteristics of people who have built up their own businesses is that they start off with a core belief that they can do it. It isn't a question of finding reasons why it can't be done, but you know that you have to jolly well do it. But what I'm not sure of is whether that is a characteristic only of entrepreneurs if you define entrepreneur as someone who starts his own business in a risk situation or whether you need to have a wider definition of entrepreneur or use a different word. For instance, if I think of somebody like . . . Pat Sheehy, who is chairman and chief executive of BAT Industries now, you cannot in a classic definition call him an entrepreneur because he started off as a branch manager in BAT and finished off as chairman and chief executive of a huge – fundamentally in the end a managerial company, it was so large. However, you would say of him, he is someone who has a mastery of the situation, or, in my sense, he will just say, 'It can be done, it must be done, it will be done.' It rather depends upon what you are starting off your definition of entrepreneur with. Now you could say of Pat Sheehy that the step from being one of a thousand branch managers of BAT to becoming the chief executive was itself an entrepreneurial exercise. But all I am saying is don't narrow the definition.

Sir Mark was asked if he was still fired with enthusiasm about entrepreneurial activity, now that he has reached the top. He describes his enthusiasm for his work, not so much for the sake of power but as an exercise, an intellectual challenge:

> Well it all depends you see, I suppose, you've got to decide what it is that fired you. If you are fundamentally driven by power, then your enthusiasm never wanes because you never have enough power. I'm not; I have a strong desire to be in control of my own destiny and I've got . . . I'm driven more than anything else by the intellectual challenge. Which comes out of being a lawyer and then going into business, which I hadn't originally chosen to do. It was just coming to live in this country. I had to go into something so I went into business. I sort of matched myself against other people running companies and I wanted to

win in that sense. I certainly like winning, but I'm not very strong on power. And for that reason, when my own business was taken over by a large multinational, I no longer felt proprietorial.

Moreover, even before it was taken over – in fact, it wouldn't have been taken over if I had not felt this way. I'd felt that . . . I had been in the same job for almost twenty-five years. . . . I started up Abbey Life 27 years ago and the company grew. But fundamentally I was doing the same job. Now, if you've got a sufficiently strong power drive then either you are going to push your frontiers very, very wide or you can have such a voracious appetite for your company to swallow up everything else that it doesn't matter how many years you go on. I happen not to have taken this path, I've just, as I say, had a more intellectual interest, plus a desire to win, plus a certain amount of monetary motivation as well. But none of them were voracious, in the sense that many entrepreneurs would see it. If you wanted to classify entrepreneurs I would put another classification even amongst what you call the elite. Some people are voracious; it may have to do with power and is often correlated with a degree of ruthlessness, which I for one, haven't got. And I think that the two are also related. If you are power mad then you are more ruthless, if you are not you are eventually going to run out of steam, and I certainly have.

Sir Mark was asked to reply to the suggestion that some studies had found entrepreneurs to be relatively poor managers.

I think that is a generalization. I can think of many entrepreneurs of whom that is true, but I think you are playing with words. If you say the entrepreneur is a person who has wonderful ideas, but does not have the organizational ability to go with them, then you have defined your own thing. I can think of one entrepreneur who surely lay awake at night thinking up ways of how he could do things the whole time. But his greatest strength was detailed nuts and bolts management – a chap called Donald Gordon who built up a huge insurance and banking operation in South Africa. I think there is a danger that entrepreneurs won't have follow-through but it doesn't follow. Let me put it a slightly different way around. I would take the point that an entrepreneur is unlikely to have the patience and attention to detail that good management is all about and therefore he is unlikely to stay the course of doing that detailed management. And that is why among the most successful entrepreneurs, although I haven't traced them through, you will probably find that there was a number two that they got into partnership with fairly early on, who did the nuts and bolts. You do see a lot of that, and that enables the colourful entrepreneur to concentrate on what he wants to do. Otherwise he does get bogged down in the management side.

In our search for the most significant talents, Sir Mark was asked what, in his opinion, was his greatest entrepreneurial talent. His reply was extremely succinct: 'Communication!'

We were interested in discovering if personal ambition was a well developed personality trait in independent entrepreneurs. When Sir Mark was questioned along these lines he replied:

No, I still see myself as ambitious, but with a very important proviso: that I don't have an unlimited appetite for power or whatever it is. I'm ambitious now to do something else. It doesn't have to be something bigger than I've done before. What is certainly true, on the money side, is that if you have made a lot of money once in one type of thing, it would be very difficult to go into something else where the money that came out of it was one-twentieth or something like that. Because your view of what is the measure of your success has been formed by that. You could turn it into some sort of community work. I have a joint chair with Hector Laing, something called the Per Cent Club, which is a thing which he conceived, but he wasn't able to get it off the ground. I got together with him and we did it together. I did the nuts and bolts, if you like, and the selling . . . or communicating. It's an idea of going to the top 200 companies and saying: you only give one-fifth of 1 per cent of your profits to charity or the community, so that's the Per Cent Club. Hector Laing was very well connected but he never closed on these people, so we got together and we started off with a half a dozen companies and we are now up to 120 of the top 200 companies. That is a tremendous sense of achievement. If I was to give up business a couple of things like that would be well worth doing. It's a valid point to say that, having achieved the top 120, I'm not enjoying the next 80 so much, so I've got in somebody else to take on that sort of responsibility. You don't need money. But if there is going to be money, then it's got to be enough to make it sensible.

Sir Mark was asked about how difficult it had been for him to establish an insurance company in the UK, and if there were barriers to market entry erected by the established insurance companies:

No, they didn't even take it seriously. Call it lucky if you like, but I had chosen an industry where the management were so non-entrepreneurial and at the same time an industry in which there was a potential for revolution.

How did you select this particular niche in the market?, we asked.

That was luck too, if you like. I was practising law in South Africa. I decided that I wanted to come and live in this country. It wasn't practical to start practising law again. I had done a lot of legal work for a South African insurance company, Liberty Life, and talking to Donald Gordon, who had founded it, I said, 'I'm thinking of starting in London, looking for things I could put together', and he said, 'Why don't you open a branch for our company?' So I said, 'Well, it doesn't really make any sense opening a branch. You made a successful life assurance company, it's worth my having a look whether I could start a new life company in the UK. Would you put some money into it?' So they put some money in and they gave me the opportunity to go and spend a few months in his office to see how to run a life company. So again, it wasn't a matter of analysing the whole market and looking at 30 sectors and deciding which one had a gap. It was a field in which I had had some interest. My father had been a successful life assurance salesman and manager. I had done a lot of work for these school friends; add to that, that there was a lot of opportunity in the UK. As it turned out, I had recognized that marketing was done very badly in this country, so that was the gap. What turned it into an enormous success was a new product, a new opportunity, that came through later. And I was surrounded by a lot of relatively inert companies in insurance.

We wanted to find out if Sir Mark had suffered 'the purgatory of entrepreneurship', that is, the period preceding recognition of one's entrepreneurial talents:

Oh yes, it wasn't terribly long, it was only a couple of years because. . . . The first eighteen months was absolute hell, then I developed along this new unit-link concept and started to find my way. One of the reasons why it wasn't as long for me as it might otherwise have been is something to hold against me in the entrepreneur stakes, if you like. That is, I sold out very early. After about two or three years of Abbey Life some Americans came along and were introduced to me, and said, 'Would you like to run a company for us and we will take over your existing company?' As it happened, a brother-in-law of mine who is an entrepreneur in Israel, walked around with a burst appendix for three days without realizing it and nearly died and I spent two weeks next to his bedside. Then I came back to this country and, having said no to one or two other approaches before, I said: I'm not going to battle about this. I started this company because I wanted a job. If someone takes it over I'll get a bigger job. So, I'm illustrating the fact that I wasn't interested in the money side of it, but I wanted to run a show, and have a good job and a sense of achievement from it. Then I had the backing of a very large organization so that made the agony much easier. We had a lot of success. After about five years of building up Abbey Life to be a very large firm, I had an argument with them – it was over independence really. I left and started a new company, Hambro Life, but by that time I was so well established as a name that a lot of people came to me. It was a very easy thing. It wasn't so entrepreneurial second time around.

Did Sir Mark think about the possibility of catastrophic financial failure?

The answer is: sometimes yes. That is why, in the end, we sold out to BAT. I had always had as one of my guiding principles to look out for catastrophe. When Hambro Life was three years old, and had made a million pounds in its third year, it was going on extremely well as if nothing could stop it. We did a projection that showed we would do £5 million profit within three years, and so on. I called my top team in for a day and I said: fine, these projections show how well things are going to go. I want to sit here and make a list – a Doomsday list – of everything that could go wrong; and we made a list of 13 things. Then I said: let's divide them into things which we cannot do anything about, and those which we can, we give up 25 per cent of our profit in the next three years to avoiding, and so on. We identified some things, such as bad publicity by our sales force, and so we poured a hell of a lot of money into training and upgrading our sales force. As it happens, within the five years I think seven out of the thirteen catastrophes actually happened. There was a stock market collapse, a property collapse, and Hambro's Bank got into trouble, and so on. So I'm very conscious of risk. I believe that any corporate plan would look at vulnerability but I put vulnerability very high on the risk agenda. So the answer is, yes, I worry.

Finally, Sir Mark was asked to describe any shaping events or significant happenings in his life.

Well, it was undoubtedly the decision to leave South Africa. There is no question that if I had stayed in South Africa I would still be at the Bar now. I would probably be a QC or a judge or something like that. Because that was my career ambition. I couldn't conceive of anything more fulfilling than being at the Bar. Within a year of leaving it, I felt, with hindsight, that it was very limiting because you were just fiddling about with papers. But it was the decision to leave South Africa that presented me with the requirement of finding the solution of what I was going to do with my life. That was half of it, if you like. Add to it I had had this relationship with a life assurance company: that gave me the hook to go into business, which I wouldn't have done otherwise. I didn't have any money, I didn't know anybody. I wouldn't have gone and started a corner shop or anything else but this was an opportunity to go into business in a field where I had some experience.

Teresa Gorman, MP

The main problem that women entrepreneurs in our research seem to have is men. Teresa Gorman explains the problems which she sees as dogging female entrepreneurs operating in a predominantly male environment. Her solution to the 'man' problem is – don't employ them! And if you must, keep a close eye on them and make sure they don't have any great power in the organization or they will try to upstage you!

> The main problem that women have to overcome is asserting themselves, especially in a room full of men. Women, you see, are trained not to be assertive and even though, like me, you are considered to be so, it's still difficult. In this place [the House of Commons] you can sit and listen to a debate and want to intervene but you just can't bring yourself to do it – for fear of rejection. Women take it personally. You have something to say but you are brought up to believe that little girls are seen and not heard. It's very difficult for a woman to overcome the indoctrination that you go through as a child.

Gorman goes on to argue that:

> As an employer, I tried once or twice employing men in senior positions but they always regarded the job as a means to extend their own standard of living, putting their personal interest above that of the company. They would stay late to make all their own personal calls, they would stretch their expenses and car allowances and they regarded the business, which I had worked hard to develop, as some 'horn of plenty', to give them a better standard of living over and above what they were earning. The women I employed were completely different: they were fair with me and I was fair with them. They were pleased to be working for me and responded much better to friendly treatment and very rarely took advantage of it. Generally speaking, the working atmosphere was much more important to them than just the money. They were far more loyal. In the end, as an employer, I gave up employing men except for driving vans and cutting the grass.

Finally, Teresa Gorman says,

> The determination to achieve in a woman must be much stronger than in

a man because nobody expects a woman to achieve much more than domesticity. The obstacles you come up against as a woman are profound – no one encourages you in the way they encourage a boy or a man – to take a chance and be more forceful. Being taken seriously by your bank manager even in this place [the House of Commons] is very difficult.

Entrepeneurial careers

In the case of the elite independent entrepreneurs, it is almost axiomatic that they will have faced challenges and overcome difficulties in building up their businesses. All showed evidence of extreme resilience and the ability to bounce back from catastrophic situations. Forty-six per cent of the entrepreneurs and 5 per cent of intrapreneurs had experienced complete financial collapse, sometimes more than once, but all had regrouped and started again, treating the event as a learning experience. A prime example is Jeffrey Archer discussing his financial collapse:

> they got away with 8 million . . . I couldn't give a damn, entrepreneurs don't give a damn . . . [you have to] stand up and say, 'You have made a bloody fool of yourself, now forget it, and get on with it.

And Lord Young, who recalls:

> I spent a very miserable year in 1973 when I thought I was rich and didn't know what to do. Very luckily for me the 1974 bank crash 'wiped me out'. And I woke up one morning full of the joys of spring because I knew what I had to do: I had to go out and earn a living again.

CASE HISTORIES – INTRAPRENEURS

The intrapreneur's career path was different from that of the entrepreneur, and it can be argued that the intrapreneur who was given responsibility for the stewardship of the family business found it that much more difficult.

Earlier we saw that entrepreneurs had experienced significant happenings fairly regularly during their careers. However, only 5 per cent of the intrapreneurs recalled such events in their career experiences, no doubt because a large majority (13 of the 19 who responded to this question) had, in fact, been 'born into' successful organizations. Their development had been along linear career paths that had been far less turbulent than those of the entrepreneurs. This doesn't mean that they were less stressful, and we do not wish to give the impression that only the entrepreneurs suffered 'the purgatory of entrepreneurship' in their climb to the top. Far from it.

Michael Guthrie

Some of the intrapreneurs' career paths were certainly far from smooth. One example is that of Michael Guthrie, who headed up the Mecca Organization. Guthrie is the archetypal dedicated, middle-class intrapreneurial business leader. In analysing his interview, we see him slowly working his way up through the corporate hierarchy:

> I started as a trainee manager, and then went from that to assistant manager, then general manager, then to area manager to working Director to Divisional Managing Director, right the way through to Chairman, so it's all been about achievement.

Under the leadership of Guthrie, Mecca moved from being a subsidiary of a holding company, through buyout, to being an independent company listed on the London Stock Exchange. On 8 October 1986, Mecca came to the stock market with an offer of sale of 25.926 million shares. This issue was ten times over-subscribed. In December 1985 Guthrie completed the purchase of the business from Grand Metropolitan, with a £95 million institutionally led management buyout. Mecca today is one of the UK's leading leisure groups. Its three major divisions are entertainment and catering, social clubs and holiday centres, and Guthrie controlled a team of over 7,000 managers and staff.

Following the death of his father, Guthrie, while still a teenager, went to catering college to study hotel and catering management, and then joined Mecca in the early 1960s as a trainee manager.

> I'm very middle-class, we were certainly not rich but neither were we poor. . . . My father was a builder . . . . When I was at catering college, although I had sufficient money from my grant to support me, I wanted to do more things – dress better and get myself about more, which needed money – so I suppose I was motivated to work over and above the normal vocational work. I worked during the college term, evenings and weekends, right through, because I needed that additional financial support to do other things. I suppose that was quite a motivating force. Without money I couldn't do the things I wanted to do. So I would say that it started then. But I moved into the recognition mode, when I really started work. You get promotion by being recognized and you get recognized by doing an exceptionally good job and that's what achievement is all about. . . . Catering colleges back in the sixties were very much orientated to the traditional hotel and restaurant world, still a very unsociable-hours activity but then it was even more so. So frankly when we came out from our course, many of us felt we had had enough of it. Whereas going into the institutionalized branch of catering which was

related to commerce and hospitals or banks or things of that nature, it was a more of a nine-to-nine operation.

And so misguidedly, I took my first trainee manager's job with the University of London and I was bored out of my tiny mind. So I then wrote off to all the catering companies and told them that I was the best thing since sliced bread, and God's gift to catering – as all 18-year-olds coming out of college think. And I was interviewed by a lot of companies and the one I thought held the greatest challenge and prospects was Mecca. I felt that they had a tremendous culture about doing things well: whether it be in the function business or in any field they touched, the customer is always right. They had an obsessional attitude to those values and that is what inspired me early on.

David Jones

David Jones explains what it was like to work his way to the top in a major commercial organization. Here he describes how he started up the intrapreneurial ladder.

I walked into his office. He was sat behind a big desk with his feet up, smoking a great big Monte Christo cigar. I said to him, 'I understand that Mr X might be leaving the company. I would like you to know that I can do his job, because frankly I'm doing it already.' He looked up at me and said, 'Would you shut the door on your way out please.' That was all he said. I walked out of his office and thought, hell, I've blown that one! He came into my office at 8.30 the next morning and said, 'Do you think you can do that job?', and I said, 'Yes, I think I can.' He said, 'OK, you've got six months to prove it.' That, if you like, is the guy that gave me my break and he has supported me ever since and we have had great fun working together.

Even when Jones had become established, it was not all smooth sailing. In this passage, we see his doubts and nagging fears which underlie his skill and apparent confidence. The fears that Jones suffered are experienced by us all. He talks about the confidence you need to be in the big league:

The company once built the most advanced warehouse in the country. In fact, we are building one now and we are spending £50 million on it, it will be the biggest one in Europe. The chairman said to me, 'I want you to go up and be Managing Director and sort out this warehouse problem.' I had never worked in a warehouse in my life. I said, 'David, I don't know too much about warehousing.' He said, 'I know that, and you know that, but don't let anyone else know it.'

My job at the moment is [pause] I run a chain of newsagents and tobacconists, I run a holiday company, I run a mail order company and I help George [Davies] to run NEXT. What I mean is, I walk into a board meeting of my tobacconists which has a turnover of about £200 million annually, and I haven't got a clue how to run any one of those things. I know that I've sat down with six people that know more than I'll ever know. So you have got to go in there and be confident, because at the end of the day they look upon you as though you are God Almighty. I mean, you haven't got to let them down.

Sir Antony Pilkington

Sir Antony Pilkington, born 20 June 1935, is the chairman of Pilkington PLC. His rise to the top of his family firm demonstrates dramatically the different paths followed by entrepreneurs and intrapreneurs in achieving their goals. Groomed early for leadership, he followed a linear career path.

He was educated at Ampleforth College, York, and at Trinity College, Cambridge, where he obtained an MA in History. This was followed by two years military training as a commissioned officer in the Coldstream Guards, which laid the foundation for his move into the family firm. He joined Pilkington in 1959 and after experience of United Kingdom and export flat glass sales activities, was appointed Flat Glass Division Marketing Manager in 1967, and then moved fairly rapidly through the following positions:

1968 he became Deputy Marketing Director, Flat Glass Division;
1970–1 Head of the Marketing Planning Department;
1971–2 Marketing Director, Flat Glass Division;
1972 Joint Managing Director, Flat Glass Division;
1973 Executive Director, Pilkington Brothers PLC;
1974–9 Chairman, Flat Glass Europe Division;
1979–80 Director Fibreglass Ltd;
1979–82 Director, Glass Fibre Division;
1979–81 Director, Optical Division;
1979–80 Deputy Chairman, Pilkington Brothers PLC;
1980 Chairman, Pilkington Brothers PLC, changed to Pilkington PLC in August 1987.

He was awarded an Honorary Degree (Doctor of Laws) by the University of Liverpool in 1987. In 1988 he was commissioned Deputy Lieutenant of Merseyside, and received his knighthood in the 1990 Queen's Birthday Honours List.

A brief history of the company will give some idea of its magnitude, and the burden of responsibility placed upon the shoulders of the single family member, whose job it is to maintain the family dynasty, and operate the firm successfully throughout his stewardship.

In brief, Pilkington PLC is the world's leading glass company, operating either exclusively or with local partners in fifteen countries. It is a typical example of the long-established, innovative, manufacturing family firm. Originally established in May 1826 as the St Helens Crown Glass Company, to produce window (sheet) glass by the Crown, and later the Cylinder, method it broke with glassmaking tradition in 1876, branching out into plate glass manufacture.

By the end of the First World War, Pilkington had become the major British flat glass producer with an extensive sales operation throughout the Empire and the 'old' dominions. In the 1930s, by acquiring a licence to toughen glass and joining with Triplex Safety Glass Co. Ltd, Pilkington entered the flourishing motor vehicle trade.

In 1959, after seven years of development, Pilkington announced the invention of Float Glass – a new way of making perfectly flat, distortion-free glass by floating molten glass on a bath of hot metal. With this development the world's flat glass technology took its most revolutionary step forward. The float glass process, unlike previous developments in flat glass manufacture, did not simply evolve from its predecessors but was a fundamental advance based on new technology. When announced, the new method of production made every plate glass factory in the world virtually obsolete. The process was invented by Sir Alistair Pilkington and has been licensed to thirty-five manufacturers in twenty-nine countries. Over 105 float glass plants are currently in operation. The royalties alone have earned the company nearly £400m. (1986).

True, the modern day success of Pilkington PLC is built on its method of making high-quality flat glass, but running parallel with this invention is the acute business acumen developed by the Pilkington family over the past 168 years.

It took Sir Antony twenty-one years to reach the top of his family firm. This point is sometimes missed when we read of members of established family firms being born with a silver spoon in their mouth. Silver spoons maybe, but the City is unforgiving, even in a world recession. Pilkington PLC has suffered over the last couple of years. Profits in the 1991–2 financial year were reduced and in the past four years the company has cut several thousands from its workforce. The chairman's penthouse office in the Pilkington Building in St Helens is, as Sir Antony has said, 'at times an extremely lonely place'. Nevertheless, Sir Antony's family is still the 122nd richest in Britain.

Martin Laing

Martin Laing is another intrapreneur who heads up his family's long established civil engineering firm. Mr Laing was asked if he could identify the traits that make a successful business leader, and how he would define the attributes necessary to achieve career success:

> I don't know . . . but I think the willingness to work hard has a lot to do with it and not just nine to five. Then there is the willingness to put yourself out for other people. And to do things that other people may not want to do. For me, I was just continuing the process . . . I just wanted to learn more things. . . .
>
> Education is obviously the number one. Then you have got to be able to speak – that doesn't mean that you have to speak with a posh accent; you have to be able to communicate. To me, that's far more important than having read the natural sciences. Speaking is the first demonstration of somebody's capability, to anybody. I think the educational side is important: every parent should try to make sure their children get the best education. Obviously one wants some people to have some kind of scientific background or learning.

Earlier in this chapter we mentioned the 'purgatory', the hardship, the struggle, and the effort required of the entrepreneur to 'make it' in the business world. We indicated that these 'shooting stars' were not the only ones who suffered and had problems. For example, Martin Laing talks about the problems and the stress associated with running his big family firm, and how he still remains motivated:

> I've been through periods when I've got really pig sick with just that [having his judgement questioned]. After all, I'm the chairman, it's just got to be accepted. The family owns the business.
>
> I said earlier that you just have to have professionals, managers to fill in the weaknesses. I have all these ideas and somebody has to make sense of them. It's all very well having the ideas, but you have to understand that some of them aren't going to fly! You have to recognize the logic of *why*. You've got a board of experienced people and you've got them there because of their experience. Now, if you say you want to make widgets, they will say we don't want to make widgets, there's no point in making widgets, somebody else makes wonderful widgets.

We asked: 'So what motivates you today?'

> I honestly don't know . . . I had a major operation in October, I had a lung operation. I think that made me take stock of life. So I said that I

wouldn't do so much – but that didn't last very long. I suppose I just enjoy the privilege that I have in my situation of meeting people, I think that's really what it is. I suppose the driving force is still the desire for learning. I am still learning every day.

In terms of planning his career, he contends:

I'm a visionary, and long-range man, myself. . . . The only part that I planned was, I suppose, going into estate management, which is really property development, and then going overseas. That was my planning . . . .

I did have the ability to foresee that the 'Greens' were coming you might say. . . . We set up an environmental division five years ago. But that was only because in my position I was lucky, and I can go around the world and I can meet people and, in the words of Tom Peters, 'I'm a great creative swiper': I pinch ideas from other businesses. The reason Tony Berry might say he operated short-term is because it was his actual business . . . it was his baby! I'm fourth generation so there's a difference and I still feel a tremendous responsibility for it. I have professional managers now, whereas before, when it was my grandfather starting, he did everything: it was his. Now as business grows it becomes more complicated. No single individual can possibly have all the necessary attributes. What we have all got to do is to recognize our weaknesses and make sure that we have got people who can fill those gaps.

Julian Smith

Julian Smith is an intrapreneur, one of the Smith family who founded W.H. Smith in the nineteenth century. How did his career path develop? And did he have any desire to work at anything else when he was a young man?

this was a family business for a long time, and I suppose my father had hopes rather than expectations for me. Certainly there was never any pressure on me to come into the business, it was my own choice . . . .

I was offered a regular commission in the Navy at the end of my National Service, and I think that is probably the only other thing I would have done.

Julian Smith was, until recently, External Affairs Director of W.H. Smith. He was born in September 1932 and educated at Eton College. Being 'born into' the family, his linear career path is fairly typical. His career with W.H. Smith Ltd began in 1950 but was interrupted almost immediately by National Service which he spent in the Royal Navy, leaving in 1952 with the rank of sub-Lieutenant. He returned to W.H. Smith in 1953 and spent the following four years gaining experience in many aspects of the business, after which he spent a year in Canada doing a variety of jobs, including selling and working in a copper mine. Returning to the UK in 1958, Smith became Northern Sales Manager of a W.H. Smith subsidiary selling a shop-fitting system.

In 1960 Smith took up the appointment of Assistant Retail Director and was involved in the overall management of all W.H. Smith retail branches. This covered all aspects of management, but he carried particular responsibility for the capital expenditure programme. Five years later he was appointed to the board of W.H. Smith & Son Ltd as Services Director responsible for all export activities, transport and head office services.

In 1967 Julian Smith was appointed Staff and Training Director and remained in this job until 1979, having responsibility for all personnel and training policies throughout the W.H. Smith Group. In 1970 he was responsible for the acquisition, equipping and establishing of a new Training College near Abingdon and for the amalgamation under one roof of all the Group's central training activities involving both management and skills training. Projects included the successful installation of the Hay/MSL Job Evaluation Programme and a major revision of appraisal and reward systems. Smith was appointed to the Board of W.H. Smith & Son Holdings PLC in July 1974 while continuing his role of Staff and Training Director of W.H. Smith & Son Ltd. During this period (from 1972 to 1983) he was also Chairman of the subsidiary company, W.H. Smith Advertising Ltd, operating in the field of outdoor advertising contracting.

In 1979 Smith was appointed to the newly created role of External Affairs Director with a brief covering the interface between the company and the outside world. This involves political relations, the company's arts sponsorship programme, the overseeing of all charitable giving and devising and running the company's programme of community involvement.

Julian Smith is a member of the London Regional Council of the CBI, a member of the General Committee of the Bible Society and a director of Project Fullemploy, a charitable body sponsored by the business community to provide realistic and effective training for disadvantaged young people.

Mr Smith was asked how he would define the attributes necessary to achieve career success.

I suppose the first thing that you need is the widest possible experience of what the job involves. Beyond that, in order to get near the top in any company you need to have a far wider knowledge than any specific job you are likely to be asked to do. You need to understand, not only the company on a broad front, but in particular. Anybody joining the company from outside, the first thing they really have to focus on is what I call the company's tribal customs, because they are always different and if you don't understand the tribal customs then you are never going to fit, and unless you fit you are never going to succeed. So you need to know the company on a broad front. You need to know the environment in which the company operates, equally on a broad front. In a sense, you need to look at those things in as detached way as you possibly can, in order to be sure that you are making your own judgements. I think those are the sort of principal things that I would set out.

We asked Julian Smith if he could identify, in one sentence or so, the traits that make a successful businessperson.

I think the answer to that question has to be 'no'. I don't think that there is any one sentence that covers all businessmen. I think that all sorts of people are successful for all sorts of different reasons. Some because they are colossally imaginative, others because they are colossally hard workers and the rest somewhere in between. It would be an over-simplification to try and distil it into one sentence.

GROUP SIMILARITIES AND DIFFERENCES IN WORK HISTORIES

Based on each group's work histories, what similarities and differences have we found between the entrepreneurs' and intrapreneurs' career development paths?

Motivation

Both groups are highly self-motivated and they continually need to satisfy some desire to achieve, not so much for the sake of social recognition or prestige, but to satisfy an inner feeling of personal accomplishment, something that wealth alone cannot satisfy. This need to be motivated, at a relatively high level, applies to entrepreneurs more than intrapreneurs, although there are exceptions. Consolidating one's position; pausing to catch one's breath; taking stock – all concepts used by the intrapreneur – are not in the vocabulary of the entrepreneur, but burnout sadly is. We observed several such burnouts during the writing of this book. These can be seen as 'downs', not absolute failures: like his theatrical counterpart, the entrepreneur is at 'rest' waiting for his next chance. It's doubtful if entrepreneurs know how to fail completely.

Business methodology vs innovation

Entrepreneurs – even today – are still innovative, 'self-made men', their knowledge being founded in hands-on experience. This is one reason why entrepreneurship is seen as a risky business, because so few entrepreneurs start with any experience of 'business'. Product skills they have, enthusiasm they have, the ability to sell both themselves and their product they have, but these skills are not complete business skills. They lack a basic business methodology. If their business is to grow they must surround themselves with competent business managers. Here is where the symbiotic relationship should develop between two equally competent groups: the intrapreneur and the entrepreneur.

This is illustrated by the experience of George Davies, creator of NEXT. It was lack of managerial expertise that contributed to his earlier collapse. As Davies explains,

> I had this great idea – and you can convince a lot of people if you have a great idea – but I'd never run a business in my life before. I didn't know anything about warehousing . . . about systems, I didn't know that if you didn't file correctly and people have queries you will never find that again.

Drucker (1989, p. 218) touches on a similar dilemma when he discusses management expertise:

> One important advance in the discipline of management is that both now embrace entrepreneurship and innovation . . . both have to be coordinated and work together. Any existing organization, whether a business, a church, a labor union, or hospital, goes down fast if it does not innovate. Conversely, any new organization, whether a business, a church, labor union or a hospital, collapses if it does not manage.

Drucker (1986, p. 44) explains that innovation can be seen as the instrument of entrepreneurship:

> It is the act that endows resources with a new capacity to create wealth. There is no such thing as a 'resource' until man finds a use for something in nature and thus endows it with economic value. Until then, every plant is a weed and every mineral just another rock. The penicillin mould was a pest, not a resource. Bacteriologists went to great lengths to protect their bacterial cultures against contamination by it. Then in the 1920s a London doctor, Alexander Fleming, realised that this 'pest' was exactly the bacterial killer bacteriologists had been looking for – and the penicillin mould became a valuable source.

The same holds true in fields other than science. Innovation with modest intellectual pretension may turn into a highly profitable business, or on occasion change the economic world. Drucker (1986) describes how Cyrus McCormick invented instalment buying, enabling this nineteenth-century American farmer to pay for a harvesting machine out of his future earnings rather than out of his past savings. Prior to this, the farmer had virtually no purchasing power. And, although there were plenty of harvesting machines about – not least McCormick's – the farmer had no way to pay for them. Suddenly the farmer had massive purchasing power, and the rest is history.

The entrepreneurs in our study showed great ability at innovation, but were not always good at routine management. The intrapreneurs, often with several generations of family business to safeguard, in general took few risks.

Jack of all trades

Entrepreneurs appear to possess more than one talent. It follows that upon commencement of their business, they are required to be 'all things, to all men': bookkeeper, office manager, financial controller, salesman, etc. They start small and learn because they have to. Not to learn is to become a minnow for the next market predator.

Intrapreneurs, on the other hand, enter a functioning corporation. Although they may start relatively low down on the corporate ladder, the structure is already in place; there exists a 'hole' for each 'peg'. Within the structure of the organization, intrapreneurs seem to possess a prudent flexibility, what NASA might call 'mid-course correction'. This adds to the chances of success and assists the intrapreneurs in their climb up the corporate ladder. Education allows intrapreneurs to start work as budding specialists in their chosen field. Here they score over the entrepreneur, because it is these very specialists that the entrepreneur must employ if the company is to survive and grow in the long term.

Management succession in family businesses

The sample for this research included 13 intrapreneurs who were 'born into' family businesses, and one of the areas of interest was whether an intrapreneur who is 'born into' the family business is the most competent manager for the job? Harry Levinson (1971), discussing the 'Conflicts that plague family businesses', suggests that the wisest course for any business, family or non-family, is to move to professional management. All organizations need to rear subordinates in a systematic manner, thus creating the basis for their own regeneration. Levinson knew of no family business capable of sustaining regeneration over the long term solely through the medium of its own family members. He points to several family businesses that have handled these issues and have become highly professional in their management, and suggests that family members must compete for advancement on the same terms as non-family members.

Sir Antony Pilkington explains the system in Pilkington Glass before he assumed the mantle of chairman:

> I think one of the great successes of Pilkington's and many other family firms that have survived for many generations, is that they don't allow members of the family who come into the firm to get to the top without proving themselves first . . . . We had a system of probation where members of the family came in [to the firm] and were reviewed at certain periods during their early careers, and if they weren't measuring up they were asked to go. This happened to a number of them. It was politely suggested that they find another job.

Another (anonymous) example of a family business 'vetting' procedure is the following:

> his father used to review each Christmas what his sons had done, and what his plans were for the next year. It's that sort of check that needs to be done in order to see where they come from and are going to.

Basically this approach is reflected in all the family businesses in this study.

The dramatic entrepreneurial business

In contrast with the solid structured fabric of the family business, we have the more turbulent and risky structure of the entrepreneur's business. Kets de Vries (1989) believes that 'Dramatic Firms' live up to their name in many respects. They are hyperactive, impulsive, dramatically venturesome, and dangerously uninhibited. Their leaders live in a world of hunches and impressions rather than facts, as they address a broad array of widely disparate projects. Their flair for the dramatic causes top echelons to centralize power, reserving their prerogative to initiate bold ventures independently.

According to de Vries, the dramatic firm's corporate strategy is paramount, for everything else seems to follow from the strategy as well as the decision-making used to formulate it. Boldness, risk-taking and diversification are the themes. Instead of reacting to the environment, some top entrepreneurs attempt to create their own environments, entering some markets and leaving others – initiating new products while abandoning older

Generally, these are major and bold actions. A sizeable proportion of the ns' capital is placed at risk. Continued growth is the goal. The organization's strategy is a function of its leader's needs and desire for visibility. It appears that the entrepreneur must feel he/she is on centre stage.

The problems of entrepreneurial management

One of the independent entrepreneur's problems appears to be the inability to 'let go' the reins of the firm once he has achieved his goal. Kets de Vries (1977), writing about the millionaires who appear in *Fortune* magazine, points out that stories of the bold entrepreneur finally succeeding and overcoming nature may have a different ending. Frequently, he says, 'there is an epilogue added to these fairy tale endings where the, "and they lived happily ever after theme", is missing'. He suggests that there can be another side to the entrepreneur, one in which he emerges as an anxious individual, a non- conformist and poorly organized. De Vries says that the entrepreneur is no stranger to self-destructive behaviour. He argues that, within the organ- ization, power which depends on the proximity to the entrepreneur is constantly changing and creates a highly uncertain organizational environ- ment. This state of affairs contributes to a highly politically charged atmosphere, where changing coalitions and collusions are the order of the day. The suprastructure is poorly defined: a formal organization chart is outdated by the time it is drawn. It basically resembles a 'spider's web', with the entrepreneur at the centre constantly changing loyalties and keeping subordinates in a state of confusion and dependence.

The organization usually has a poorly defined or poorly used control and information system; there is an absence of standard procedures and rules and a lack of formalization. Job descriptions and job responsibilities are poorly defined. This contributes to a high incidence of role conflict and role ambiguity, leading to low job satisfaction, low self-confidence, a high degree of job-related tension and futility, and low confidence in the organization. Avoidance behaviour and a reduction in communication among employees also becomes systematic. Information hoarding turns into common practice and contributes to the disorganization. In addition, given the 'spider's web' structure, the number of people reporting to the entrepreneur will be large, adding to the general sense of confusion.

Kets de Vries explains that, although the entrepreneur in the initial stage of development of the enterprise may have had the ability to inspire subordinates, the mere fact of growth has complicated this process. His aversion to structure, his preference for personalized relationships and his reluctance to accept constructive criticism makes growth, with its implicit need for a more sophisticated infra- and suprastructure and greater decentralization, increasingly difficult to handle. Hoarding of information, inconsistencies in day-to-day interpretation of company policies, and reluctance to let people really know where they stand do not contribute to an efficient and effective organization. If this pattern becomes predominant it will lead to increasing inefficiency, and the eventual collapse of the organization.

WHAT ARE THE ATTRIBUTES NECESSARY TO ACHIEVE CAREER SUCCESS?

Some of our sample were almost guaranteed success by being born into the right family. For others, it was a climb from very low beginnings. What, then, are the special skills one needs to get to the top? One view suggests that it is an ability to focus narrowly on one's work. As Sir David Alliance puts it, 'it is doing what you think is important, doing it as well as you are able; this has always been part of my philosophy'. Some have a kind of second sight, taking over 'lame ducks' or bankrupt businesses. They believe they alone can make them work. In the process, they can mortgage their homes to the hilt and burden themselves with massive debts on nothing more than a hunch. They have an unquenchable belief in themselves. They seem to delight in the exercise of their skill. The wealth they achieve is just a marker in the 'game'.

Some entrepreneurs talk of knowing your limits; they believe that the entrepreneur should proceed in an orderly manner, always evaluating the 'down side'. But this phase must surely be after the firm has become established. Initially, it is doubtful if this path is followed as it suggests long/medium-range detailed planning, a methodology few entrepreneurs would recognize. Generally, the entrepreneur, according to Berry, 'rolls with the punches', and when he sees an opening he will, as Bradman says, 'go for the jugular'. Long-term planning belongs to the intrapreneur who operates the family firm. Here the aim is keeping control and successfully passing the company on to succeeding generations.

Kets de Vries (1980) argues that prior to commencing in business, entrepreneurs tend to follow a transitory career path. This pre-entrepreneurial period can be seen as a trial phase during which time the individual tests out abilities and develops latent skills. Initially, the potential entrepreneur often has no clear focus on which career to pursue and so moves from job to job discovering strengths and weaknesses. The potential entrepreneur searches for some niche, some product, some service, which can sustain him/her, and which is enjoyable and offers the entrepreneur independence and control over life. However, on starting a business, the career concept may change and stabilize.

As Teresa Gorman, MP, recalls:

> I was the only girl I knew who wanted a career – and that was to teach. And as far as I was concerned it was the only available job that was secure . . . and that I could go back to and make a reasonable career. I suppose I could have done nursing but I didn't fancy that. I was the first in my family, in what might loosely be called a profession.
>
> My father was a small businessman, so in a way I was brought up in a business atmosphere. I remember I used to help do up the wages on a Friday night on the kitchen table. Then we used to go out and pay the wages on Saturday morning. My father had a demolition business. He knocked down old houses and buildings and I loved to go out to the site. He had a yard where he used to sell the bits and pieces he had rescued from the demolition contracts: bricks, tiles, lead.
>
> My mother's parents were wholesale greengrocers. Eventually, even though I had ten years in teaching, I reverted to my natural roots, and set up a business of my own. Even as a young woman, I felt highly motivated to be independent.

Sometimes the change is created by some form of career block. Lord Archer, after following what would otherwise have been described as a steady career path, found this after his financial collapse:

> I couldn't get a job . . . but they can't stop you writing, and if you are in debt for £472,727 and you are looking for a job that there's not much chance of getting . . . I would never have written a word if I had stayed in the House of Commons.

George Davies, the architect of the high street chain NEXT, offers yet another impetus to the start of an entrepreneurial career:

> You have to want to break the mould . . . I started a holiday job at Littlewoods and Littlewoods was the sort of regime that was highly dictatorial and the strange thing is, if a place is dictatorial you either say, 'I don't go along with that lot', or you say, 'I'll show that lot'. My way of rebelling was to say 'I'll get on, I'll get above you y'know'. So within me was that feeling of I wanted to get my own back on the day . . . to win and not be kicked around.

Robert Gavron, the entrepreneurial printer, sums up the feelings of many when reflecting on the critical factors in achieving success:

> I think you have got to have the desire to do everything better today than you did the day before, metaphorically speaking, that is. I think that you have got to care about your work and not just regard it as a source of

money. I think you have got to care about the people who are working with you and not just think of them as people to exploit. And I think the same applies to the people who consume whatever it is you manufacture, if you make something, also the people who supply you. The people who provide you with the money, your shareholders. I think that you have got to genuinely care about what you are doing. For example if you are playing cricket and building a great innings your interest is dealing with each separate ball. You are interested in getting through difficult phases; very occasionally you might look at the scoreboard to see how you are doing, that's what the money is – your score.

When asked to elaborate on differences between the entrepreneur and the manager; and whether they had different characteristics, Gavron replied:

These [traits] are quite different; as an entrepreneur, I think, you have to have this fundamental desire to be independent and plough your own furrow. To be a good manager is far more complicated. You've got to have objectives, you've got to be good with people, you've got to be numerate, you've got to be able to relate your actions to the bottom line. You've got to be honest – and I would put that very high – real integrity, that's what you need and, finally, you've got to be hungry. Regarding entrepreneurs . . . one thing I would subscribe to is that there are no generalizations that can be made about entrepreneurs either, they are all different and totally different styles can work just as well. The only thing that you can say about entrepreneurs is that they are rather individual people and don't tend to wear many grey suits.

EXECUTIVE SUMMARY

In this chapter we have presented some case histories of prototypical entrepreneurs and intrapreneurs. From these we have made a number of broad generalizations concerning their similarities and differences. Both groups show very high levels of motivation and need to achieve. The intrapreneurs, however, have a generally more cautious approach to life, showing more concern to develop their businesses stage by stage, consolidating each step as they go. The entrepreneurs show a higher level of innovation and risk-taking, together with rather greater versatility.

The main problem of the older family business, within which the intrapreneurs tend to be located, is ensuring smooth top management succession. Many of these organizations employ a variety of vetting mechanisms to ensure the suitability of those family members who are being promoted to senior positions. The entrepreneurial companies are, by contrast, far more turbulent. The main problem in this type of organization is lack of control and communication, which arises from the mercurial temperament of the entrepreneur at the top.

3   Childhood

It is widely recognized that childhood experience can have significant effects on later life. As early as the fifth century BC, Plato stated in *The Republic*: 'The first step, as you know, is always what matters most, particularly when we are dealing with those who are young and tender. That is the time when they are taking shape and when any impression we choose to make leaves a permanent mark.' But it is probably Sigmund Freud who has done more than any other writer to propagate this view. In *An Outline of Psycho-Analysis* he states: 'analytic experience has convinced us of the complete truth of the common assertion that the child is psychologically father of the man and that the events of the first years are of paramount importance for the whole of subsequent life'.

Growing up can be seen, in large part, as an imitative process. Bruce (1976) suggests, for example, that the developing child looks for somebody to model him/herself on. The child's primary experience comes from the immediate environment, which is generally the home, where the predominant influence is usually the father and/or mother. Devereaux (1969) have shown that having a supportive parent leads to an 'internal' locus of control, that is, the individual believes that the rewards they receive in life result from forces within themselves; they feel that they can influence the course of events. Personal destiny such individuals see as coming from within, and they are driven by their own internal forces. Such 'internals' are considered to be relatively self-reliant and to want independence and autonomy. In contrast, other people have an 'external' locus of control: they see the rewards they get in life as coming from forces outside themselves – from luck, fate or significant others. Devereaux suggests that having overprotective and controlling parents encourages the development of an external locus of control. Most people, of course, fall somewhere between these two extremes.

A study by Shapero (1975), using Rotter's Internal–External (I–E) Locus of Control scale, comparing business school students and entrepreneurs, indicated that the students were much more 'external' than the entrepreneurs. This finding is important, since one of the characteristics which is of interest in helping define the difference between entrepreneurs and intrapreneurs may be their degree of external/internal control. There is support for this from other studies. Cox and Cooper (1988) and White (1989) have shown that an important personality characteristic of entrepreneurs is the degree to which they feel they can affect the world around them.

So it seems not unreasonable to start the search for the determinants of a successful business career, whether as entrepreneur or intrapreneur, by looking at events in early life which seem to have been important to the individuals concerned, and which they see as having had a clear influence on their later career. This approach is further supported by Gilder (1986), who argues that entrepreneurs are nearly always driven by familial roles and obligations.

SUPPORTIVE PARENTS

We found evidence to suggest that the parents of our interviewees were, in general, extremely supportive. The parents of entrepreneurs were usually more supportive than the parents of intrapreneurs. This is significant because, like Devereaux, we also found that entrepreneurs had a significantly greater 'internal' locus of control than intrapreneurs. There was some evidence to suggest that parents wanted control over their teenage children – especially daughters – but in general, our data indicates that neither entrepreneurs nor intrapreneurs were overprotected as children, but that each group had received considerable parental support, mainly from the mother. This can be illustrated by a number of examples from our study.

Tony Berry, managing director and founder of the largest employment agency in the world, Blue Arrow PLC, came from a poor, working-class background. His father took on a part-time job as a bookmaker's clerk to send his son to a 'good' school. Berry's childhood was one of a loving, caring relationship with both his parents. He reflects on his childhood and his relationship with his parents in the following way:

> I really would like my mum and dad to be alive today to see it [his success], I'd love that. I must say to you, God, I'd give everything if they could just see my success . . . . They were marvellous people, they had no money but they gave me the best of everything.

Owen Oyston, entrepreneur owner of Red Rose Radio, Blackpool Football Club and a large communications empire, is another typical example. Oyston had been ill for years during his youth, and had missed most of his schooling. It might have been thought he would receive some sympathy from his mother when he was reluctant to get a job, but, in fact, she pressed him all the harder:

> Remember, I never had much schooling because of illness, so I was treated like an idiot. It was my mother who kept on at me to do something. My mother was the driving force: she created the uneasiness about my not working, the pressure for the need for me to really produce something and prove to the world that you had something in you . . . . Then came the realization that I could do something, I could act. It was a combination of things that set me off in a business career.

Jeffrey Archer, millionaire bestselling author, recalls: 'My mother is mentally energetic . . . and immensely enthusiastic. I have inherited some considerable amount of her determination.'

Entrepreneur Peter de Savary reflects on his childhood:

> My mother was very influential . . . she has been an enormous anchor or rock in my life. No matter what personal trouble, or business troubles or emotional troubles I have gone through, my mother is always there. She is very important to me.

These are simply a few examples showing the caring relationship which existed between parent and child in the case of many leading entrepreneurs. Many offered the observation that their parents' guidance and concern was in large part responsible for their later successes in life.

We found that intrapreneurs' responses were similar, although less graphic than those of the entrepreneurs. Julian Smith, a director and family member of W.H. Smith, the newsagent, recalls: 'I would say that I had an extremely good relationship with my parents, extremely happy.' Martin Laing, head of the John Laing Engineering Group explains, 'It was a good relationship. My parents were very busy, so I didn't see much of them. I was born during the war, so father was away . . . I guess I was closer to my mother than my father.'

Sam Whitbread, who heads the brewery group of that name, recalls that he was closer to his mother, but respected his father. Whitbread goes on to say that he was much influenced by his father's sense of duty. This was also the case with Norman Burrough, whose family founded Beefeater Gin. He enjoyed a close relationship with both parents, but feels that to some extent his father and brother influenced the way in which he developed.

In contrast to the male entrepreneurs, several women business leaders were not nearly so positive about the help received from their parents – especially their mothers. One entrepreneur, although influenced by her mother, objected to her narrow focus. Her aim, it appears, was to channel her daughter into becoming a hairdresser. The purpose of this orientation was to give her daughter a degree of freedom and independence, should her marriage fail in later years. Several women interviewees talked of conflicting and different experiences to those of their male counterparts. Typically, Teresa Gorman MP, an innovator and designer of scientific equipment, explains:

> It was really my mother's encouragement that I should be independent. This was based on the marriage situation in our household. They [my parents] weren't happily married. My mother couldn't have left my father, because she couldn't have supported herself and the children. It's not like today, many a woman can leave and manage because the state helps. In those days, nobody helped you, so my mother was stuck in an unhappy marriage with three small children. She always impressed upon me the importance, as a woman, not to be dependent on a man. I grew up not knowing quite what that meant, but knowing that's what I must

---

Sir Antony Pilkington on parental influence:

I think that it is difficult to look back and ascribe your motives to the influence of your family over a long period of time. But there is no question that if you are born into a family business, as you grow up you get to know a lot about it.

My father was in Pilkington except during the war, when he was a soldier. He was a director of the company, so I knew a great deal about it . . . even when I was at school. I would listen to my parents talking about Pilkington's in the evenings.

After I had finished my two years National Service and three years at university, I had to look around and decide what job to do. I had no particular vocation in mind on coming down from university, and therefore Pilkington was the obvious choice. If I had had a burning desire to be a doctor or to join some other profession, I would not have joined Pilkington. So I found the decision crept up on me. I came to the conclusion that it would be madness not to join a business which was not only started by my family, but was also a private company. I concluded that at least I should give it a try because it was there; it was interesting, and I knew a lot of people in it, and so I joined Pilkington's.

Harold Woolf speaking on the influence of his father:

My father wanted me to have a profession because he grew up with a very poor background, his parents being Russian immigrants. We never starved as children, we always had food, and funnily enough, I was never really short of money. I could always make a few quid selling things . . . but by any standards we were not rich but very ordinary Soho folk. He [my father] said, 'I want you to have a profession because with a profession I think you are set in life.' Well, I said, 'I don't like office work', so he said, 'Why don't you become a chemist, because it's shop work', so I said, 'Fine' and I became a chemist to please him.

I grew up in Soho and went to a very small local school. Later when I qualified [as a chemist] and worked the year to get my apprenticeship over, the day I qualified I left and looked to find a business. My father said to me, 'Don't you think you should have a job?' and I said, 'No'. If I had a job I would never find a business. I never had anything in mind other than owning my own business.

be. As for my mother, she was very much an influence on me because her aim in life was to see that her daughters were independent. She always pressed on me the need for a woman to have a job. This was her idea of a safety net if you were in a duff marriage. I never received formal academic encouragement from my parents because neither of them thought it was worth spending much money educating their daughters. As a matter of fact, I educated myself in defiance of their wishes really, by borrowing money and going off to college and qualifying as a teacher and, later on, doing an external university degree. I never had any help academically. They thought the way your career should go was that you leave school and get a job, train and be a hairdresser . . . or something like that, so that you could earn your living. In our household, earning your living consisted of running your own business. We didn't think about working for other people. My parents didn't look at life like that.

The intrapreneur, Emma Nicholson, MP, a computer software expert, also recalls that she

received no encouragement and some discouragement. My parents wanted me to be happily married with children in a comfortable environment and not to work. However, watching my father's political work influenced my final career choice. Watching my sister advance in music encouraged me to try hard at that as well, although I was discouraged in that, by my parents. But, basically, it was my own large inquisitiveness that triggered everything else.

Jennifer d'Abo, chairman of Moyses Stevens Investments Ltd, was one female entrepreneur who as a child enjoyed a close loving relationship with her parents. However, her role model turned out to be the entrepreneur Lionel Green, a surrogate father figure.

Basically, what we are seeing in the women respondents – Gorman, D'Abo and Nicholson – is what Silver (1986) called the three characteristics necessary to becoming an entrepreneur – dissatisfaction, energy and insight.

Marshall (1984) makes a distinction between public and private worlds, which may be applied to the mothers of some of our respondents. Marshall suggests that many women's sphere of influence is restricted to the private world, or home. Their position in this world can serve to moderate the male domination experienced within the public world of work. Marshall states that in the private arena women have the opportunity to establish their identity, skills and influence, which are recognized and valued by other family members. It is this process which appears to have been operative in the case of some of our male entrepreneurs. Positively valuing their mother's role and influence within the private sphere almost certainly gave Tony Berry, Owen Oyston, Sir Mark Weinberg, Jeffrey Archer and Peter de Savary the initiative to develop and appreciate their own abilities and strengths. However, Teresa Gorman and Emma Nicholson saw their mothers' role as a smothering, Victorian influence, and acted as a spur for both to rebel against claustrophobic attitudes. We would need a larger sample to be sure, but perhaps for female business leaders their parents' traditional attitude to sex roles acts as an obstacle to be overcome.

REBELLIOUSNESS

Obviously, further data is needed to address the true quality of the relationship between male and female progeny and supportive or controlling parents, but it is interesting to note that an inability to identify with parental figures, as in the case of Teresa Gorman and Emma Nicholson, is said to encourage the adoption of 'conformist rebelliousness'. This strategy is characterized by an ever-present urge to rebel, restrained by forces which necessitate compromise. If this conflict is unresolved the individual lives in a state of perpetual tension, the outcome of which is *stress*. Such individuals often possess controlled hostility and suspicion toward people in authority, due to their earlier perceptions of control, rejection and inconsistencies in parental actions. These problems may lead to identity confusion and difficulties with career choices.

This theme of rebelliousness is emphasized by Collins, Moore and Unwalla (1964), who regard the act of independent entrepreneurship as, 'in a sense a kind of permanent revolution which does not involve direct attack on the established citadels of power'. This acts as a safety valve for our society by channelling rebelliousness into socially acceptable activities.

A special case can perhaps be made for the author Dame Catherine Cookson. Although not a businesswoman in the traditional sense, Catherine Cookson can certainly be seen as entrepreneurial. Her success as a world-renowned author cannot be attributed to loving and supportive parents; on the contrary, her success seems to be in spite of her parents. Perhaps Cookson's rebelliousness against abject poverty, an absent father and a drunken mother were the stimuli, the psychological and social irritants, the 'pebbles in her shoes', that made her go forward just that much more quickly than most. When questioned about her relationship with her parents as role models she answered:

> I followed neither of them; in any case, I knew only one [her mother], but following my mother would have led me to her main weakness, the bottle . . . and my father; don't ask me, apply to God, for only he knows.

SEPARATION IN CHILDHOOD

A substantial body of research exists which assesses the quality of the relationship between managers and their parents. Cox and Cooper (1988) identified a theme in the literature on the effects of deprivation in childhood, and the enduring belief that this has an influence on later life. Their research found a common pattern of separation from, or loss of, a parent – particularly the father – during formative years amongst many of the chief executives whom they interviewed. It is possible that this experience may be paralleled by the remote father figure that many entrepreneurs identify with, although the element of rejection described by Kets de Vries (1977) is not present in the Cox and Cooper study.

Cox and Cooper, in their study of chief executives, suggest that the effect of the death of the father is to develop an early sense of responsibility and an ability to take charge of one's own life. If the individual is successful this also fosters the development of an 'internal' locus of control. Cox and Cooper hypothesized that it is not the event itself, but *how* the individual responds to it that determines the path he/she will take. Coping successfully with traumatic early life events, it is proposed, sets a pattern for successful coping with future events. It could be said that the chief executives have developed a sense of 'strength through adversity'.

A common theme of much of the literature which focuses on childhood is the effect of the death of a parent; as stated above, we have found that the effect seems to be to instil into the child an urgent sense of responsibility. Table 3.1 shows that 37 per cent of entrepreneurs had suffered the death of a parent while under the age of 16, whereas only 9 per cent of intrapreneurs had suffered a similar loss. The table also details the loss or prolonged 'absence of parent' against 'parents present' throughout childhood. Again, entrepreneurs are significantly more likely to have suffered a prolonged absence of one or both parents prior to age of 16.

Many interviewees commented on the loss or absence of a parent during childhood. For example, the entrepreneur Sir Mark Weinberg, founder of Abbey Life, states:

> Well, I never knew my father because I was two when he died, but he was certainly held up by my mother as a person who would have 'liked it' if I did this sort of thing. So it was a sort of remote-type role model. Certainly that was the picture that I had in mind.

The entrepreneur Sir Nigel Broackes, chairman of Trafalgar House, recalls that his father died in 1943 when Sir Nigel was 8 years of age, and that he suffered relative poverty for some time afterwards.

Godfrey Bradman, the philanthropist entrepreneur, is also typical of this group. He said about his childhood: 'once my father had gone I knew I had to do it myself . . . I saw money as the only way of buying myself out of a constant state of penury.'

Table 3.1 Childhood: experienced prolonged absence of parent

	Entrepreneurs	*Intrapreneurs*
Number	19	22
Parent died in childhood*	37%	9%
Parent absent in childhood**	58%	27%
Parent(s) present throughout childhood	5%	64%

*Death of a parent prior to the child's 16th birthday.
**Parent absent for over four years prior to the child's 16th birthday.

Lord Archer on his family background:

I'm the only child. And so I think that means that my parents concentrate a tremendous amount on me. I don't know if there is any universality out there, or any proof that is a factor. David Hemery (the Olympic gold medallist) told me one amazing fact – read his book called *Achievers* – he said that 98 per cent of us lost our father before the age of 15. I thought that was staggering and I'm talking about Gary Sobers, Jim Hanson, Jeffrey Archer, we are a sort of cross-section of achievers.

A poignant account of the death of a parent was related by the intrapreneur Francis Bailey, president of Bailey Retail:

My mother died when I was 14 but one of the things she taught me was to need her; but also to be able to get along without her. I didn't realize that she knew she was going to die and she wanted to teach me that.

Michael Guthrie, the former chairman of Mecca, one of the UK's leading leisure organizations, recalls:

My father died in his early fifties. I was only a teenager so to some extent my education suffered. My family life was not stable and I ended up going to catering college and did a three-to-four-year hotel management course.

Finally, both Lord Archer and Eddy Shah were deprived of a father figure during childhood: Archer's father was killed and Shah's father was absent for long periods. However, in later life both interviewees, as relatively young men, created great wealth for themselves. Similarly, both men suffered catastrophic financial failure after initial heady successes, but in the face of adversity both recovered, with Archer paying back every penny he owed. Both are again entrepreneurial high-flyers.

Obviously, with our relatively small sample size, the findings in Table 3.1 should be interpreted with some caution, as we do not yet know whether other less successful groups have similar background events in childhood. In some cases they do. Many children of the same generation as our sample lost or were separated from their parents during the war and many thousands were evacuated. Not all became successful entrepreneurs or chief executives. Whilst we believe that these are all significant shaping events, what may well be important is not the event itself, but how the individual responds to it by setting up a pattern of successful coping strategies to handle adversity. This point is expressed most succinctly by Cooper and Hingley (1985):

> Psychologists may see these early adverse experiences as likely to be traumatic, literally 'wounding' to the developing personality. Yet, as the physical wound produces healthy scar tissue often stronger than normal to protect the damaged area, so the personality may protect itself by defending vulnerable aspects of the psyche in similar ways by compensating through a number of defense mechanisms. Certainly, a number of those we interviewed reported feelings of strength through adversity, with the early personal trauma leading to the successful testing out of survival skills which leads to a fundamental feeling of strength, self-sufficiency and independence which some claim is useful in their later careers.

Cooper and Hingley report that there is also a deviation in the way the CEOs appear to have responded to childhood experiences when compared to the entrepreneurs. The effect of the death of their father leads to the development of an early sense of responsibility, as opposed to the rebelliousness we mentioned earlier. There is said to be an effect on the personality due to changing family relations, when the male influence is removed and the female influence asserts itself. Separation from parents on being sent to boarding-school is recalled as significant: it helped to develop independence and an ability to cope with life on their own.

Kets de Vries (1980) suggests that a central problem for entrepreneurs is their relationship with their father. The father is portrayed as a remote, rejecting and unpredictable figure who acts as a poor role model. This relationship is said to increase the likelihood of insecurity, self-esteem problems and lack of self-confidence. Kets de Vries's proposal finds support in the findings of *The Change Makers* (Cooper and Hingley, 1985), in which the individuals identify their father as a somewhat remote and distant figure. Kets de Vries (1977) describes the mother of the entrepreneur as a strong and controlling woman who keeps the family together and, to some extent, assumes the father's traditional role. This portrayal is not totally in line with the findings of Cooper and Hingley, who claim that the mother has a subtle influence, providing security and encouragement, enabling her children to succeed. Support for Kets de Vries and Cooper and Hingley comes from Hornaday and Bunker (1970) in an early study which they conducted on the nature of entrepreneurs. This also refers to deprivation during the formative years and to determination to overcome this. Many of those interviewed in our study mentioned a reaction against a father who provided either inadequate financial or emotional support.

DEPRIVATION IN CHILDHOOD: SHAPING EVENTS

Interviews with entrepreneurs (Collins *et al.*, 1964) and *The Change Makers* (Cooper and Hingley, 1985) have emphasized the importance of deprivation in childhood experiences. The main issues they discussed are overcoming hardships, for instance escape from poverty, insecurity, death of a parent, or parents who moved away from the nuclear family unit. Frequently, there is a tale of childhood deprivation which is recalled vividly, and is often thought to be significant in later development. Additional support comes from David Silver (1986), who discovered in an extensive survey of major American successes that most people were driven by conscious feelings of deprivation and guilt stemming from broken families and connections. Many had lost their fathers in childhood through death or divorce; many later lost their wives.

Of the entrepreneurs questioned in our study, 74 per cent of them could identify some significant shaping event in their childhood, whereas only 14 per cent of intrapreneurs could identify such an event. The entrepreneur, Robert Gavron, chairman of St Ives Printing, comments that the most significant event of his childhood was at public school: 'I felt I just had to

---

Harold Woolf on childhood:

I had an erratic childhood, not what I would call normal. I told you that my father was in the night club business and that doesn't lend itself too much to a good home life. I suppose I never really had a good home. I was evacuated in the war to Essex and came back just before the time of the Blitz. I lived in half a dozen different homes that were pretty awful and one of them was positively criminal. I lived down the Underground for six or nine months during the war. My schooling up to the age of say, 9, was not very good, what with changing homes and changing schools and living in very grotty circumstances. After 9 they changed from grotty to passable. Around the age of eleven I took the eleven-plus and you had a choice to go into grammar school or one of those other ones. I don't remember much about the exam. I certainly was not looked at as a guy who would pass the exam because my mother has since told me that the principal of the school said maybe I should forget about it. However, I managed to pass and go to a grammar school and one thing led to another. I was pretty crappy for the first year but the second year and the year after, I was always up in the first two or three.

escape that suffocating place . . . I hated every minute of it.' The philanthropist and entrepreneur property developer Godfrey Bradman vividly remembers one shaping event in his childhood:

> I can remember hoeing kale . . . you got tenpence per hundred yards and I can remember doing 1,200 yards and earning ten shillings, I must have been ten at the time . . . it was the period when we didn't have a shilling for the electric meter.

Finally, one respondent recalls painfully a significant event which he feels was a turning point in his life. As a boy, this particular interviewee had fallen foul of the law and had spent a short time in the Dover Remand Centre.

> It was the prison officer who broke my nose. On my being released [from remand] he shouted, 'You'll be back . . . you'll always be a second-class citizen.' I knew then that I had to do something, and I vowed never to return to that ghastly place.

It should be stressed, however, that many of these successful individuals did not look back on their childhood as depressing and unhappy; quite the reverse. Almost all of them, when asked about childhood, including those whose father or mother had died or who had been separated from their parents through divorce, separation or the war, responded quite spontaneously that it was normal and happy. Francis Bailey, who lost his mother in his childhood, reports: 'I had a very good relationship with my parents, we all lived as a family together . . . we didn't have much money but I didn't know any different, we always had enough to eat.'

THE NATURE–NURTURE DEBATE?

We have seen that childhood experiences play an important role in the development of the business leader, but it is still unclear whether leaders are born or made. McCall, Lombardo and Morrison (1988) record that some of the executives that they worked with maintained that leadership is not something that can be trained or developed: 'you have it or you don't'. Other executives act as if any clay can be moulded or shaped into an effective manager. McCall and his colleagues argue that while the research can never be definitive, sufficient evidence exists to conclude that neither the 'nature or nurture' explanation is adequate. This is an old debate in psychology.

There is little doubt that some predisposing factors are genetic. Tom Bouchard (1976) found, in his research on twins reared apart, that 61 per cent of leadership was genetically determined, or at least developed so early in life that it cannot be changed to any great extent in later years.

Support for Bouchard can be found in another study, 'All about twins', (1987), where it was found that basic intellectual capacity appeared to be in one's wiring. Bruce (1976) and Hertz (1987) suggest the predisposing factors, if not genetic, are the product of growing up – the socialization of the individual during pre-work years. What we can say is that the lessons of life's experiences begin early, with the influence of family, peers, education, sports and other events of childhood shaping the leader-to-be. Much the same is true of our interviewees.

When it comes to actual managerial and executive effectiveness, it is not possible to provide a comprehensive list of all potentially relevant characteristics and the ages at which they are acquired. Volumes have been devoted to efforts at predicting executive effectiveness by measuring personality traits, cognitive abilities and background experiences, all to little avail. More important than the modest associations between these endless lists of variables, Kotter (1982) suggests, is the unassailable fact that senior executives do not emerge fully competent. We would concur. Regardless of our respondents' genetic endowment, whatever their home life, however good their education, the business leader of multi-million-pound enterprises did not walk, without preparation, into the chairmanship. As Kotter (1982) in *The General Managers* remarks, 'it takes ten to twenty years to "grow" a general manager'.

SUPPORTIVE PARENTS: THE ABILITY TO BOUNCE BACK

Hertz (1987) explains that growing up with the acknowledgement of one's abilities from the people who matter most, one's parents, is a great incentive and a tremendous strengthener of character. From our interviews we know that Lord Young, George Davies, Gerald Ronson, Peter de Savary, Owen Oyston, Lord Archer and Tony Berry all had particularly supportive parents. Also, in later life, all had suffered catastrophic failures. Lord Young was 'wiped out' in the bank crash of 1974. Lord Archer (former MP) was scapegoated and humiliated after stories in the *News of the World* and the *Star* newspapers linked him with a prostitute. This was on top of his financial collapse, when he ended up in debt to the tune of £472,727. George Davies 'went down' twice, once with Childcare Ltd – his own company – and again with NEXT PLC, when he was removed from the board. Tony Berry was removed from his board after the Blue Arrow shares scandal. Ronson, at one time the fifth-richest man in Britain, was incarcerated in Ford open prison, only to take up the mantle of leadership upon his release and return to Heron International. Young, Archer, Berry, Ronson and Davies are all once again, leaders in their fields.

This tenaciousness, this ability to fight back when you're losing, is probably one of the entrepreneur's most necessary attributes. The polar opposite to the entrepreneurs' mastery of a situation is 'helplessness' – the perceived lack of mastery of a situation exhibited by many low achievers. The inability to perceive the connection between one's actions and their outcome has been called 'learned helplessness' (Seligman and Maier, 1975). These authors describe this as a belief that one cannot influence the production of positive events. If we could understand the precise mechanism which makes entrepreneurs like Lord Young, Jeffrey Archer, George Davies and others turn to 'mastery of the situation', as opposed to 'helplessness' when they suffered catastrophic failure, then social science would have made real strides. Indeed if we could teach others with fewer life chances to approach life in a similar way, the day-to-day crises might become the exception rather than the norm for many low achievers.

EXECUTIVE SUMMARY

Our data shows two distinct streams in terms of childhood experiences. The male entrepreneurs suffered more deprivation during childhood, but appeared to have had a closer relationship with their mothers than male intrapreneurs. Women entrepreneurs and intrapreneurs tended to show a pattern of rebelliousness against their parents. Entrepreneurs suffered the loss of a parent during their childhood considerably more often than did intrapreneurs. All business leaders have some childhood experiences in common, which generates common characteristics such as tenaciousness, ability to recover from trauma, and the need to achieve. It appears to be the reaction to a childhood trauma and not the event itself which counts in later life. That some basic intellectual capacity is genetic we do not dispute, but there is little doubt that childhood shaping events contribute significantly to developing the leaders-to-be. A combination of learning from adversity and tenaciousness in relation to early personal trauma, leading to the successful testing out of different survival hypotheses, are the elements used by business leaders to overcome failure. Entrepreneurs display a high degree of self-motivation and mastery of their environment. They demonstrate a remarkable resilience in the face of failure. Finally, parents – particularly the mother – play a most powerful role in establishing entrepreneurial action in the male child.

4   Social origins and marginalization

The social background of managers has for some time been a topic of interest to researchers. As far back as the late 1950s, Clements (1958), in a study of all managers in 28 firms in the north-west of England, found social class to be significant: 'A comparison between the social origins of the managers in the sample, and those of the general male population, suggests that the chances of young men of higher social origins successfully becoming industrial managers was considerably greater than those of lower social origins.' This finding is supported by Norburn (1985), who in a cross-cultural study of British and American corporate leaders found that British managers came from the 'professional' non-business class, whereas the US manager was more likely to come from parents with blue-collar occupations. Norburn goes on to suggest that the overall picture shows that Americans are more socially upwardly mobile, whereas social class mobility in Britain is slow, perpetuating the elite.

As socio-economic background can be seen as affecting development, there is good reason to find out whether a connection exists between entrepreneurs and intrapreneurs and their socio-economic background. Our results on elite intrapreneurs supports the findings of both Norburn and Clements, but the entrepreneurs, on the whole, come from very different backgrounds.

Our data (see Table 4.1) shows that a massive 72 per cent of elite independent entrepreneurs have working-class origins, and do not have entrepreneurial parents. In contrast, 73 per cent of the intrapreneurs had predominantly upper/middle-class backgrounds. What this demonstrates is that for entrepreneurs at least, 'class' is not a barrier to financial success. Providing the motivation is sufficient, lowly origins can be overcome. However, to be the CEO of some huge public organization, having the 'correct' social background can be an asset.

To discover that innovators and entrepreneurs can come from relatively lowly origins is not new. For Max Weber (1958), in his essays on *The*

Table 4.1 Social origins

	Entrepreneurs	Intrapreneurs
Number	25	22
Working-class origins	18 (72%)	6 (27%)
Other classes	7 (28%)	16 (73%)

Protestant Ethic and the Spirit of Capitalism, the people who epitomized the spirit of capitalism and economic enterprise were mainly self-made men. They were the upwardly mobile lower middle classes, not the more tradition-bound aristocratic entrepreneurs. The point made by Weber was that certain classes (i.e. those of the less tradition-bound self-made men) were more likely to be entrepreneurs imbued with the Protestant ethic and spirit of capitalism.

It may be reassuring for ordinary folk to know that they still have a chance to win. As Leah Hertz (1987) suggests, the successes of people from underprivileged backgrounds is always fascinating because it reinforces our belief in human ability, and promises us all a chance. The 'rags to riches' stories of self-made entrepreneurs seem all the more intriguing the lower their origins.

MARGINALIZATION

According to Mageean (1980) there are individuals who are much less than fully integrated into the society in which they live. She explains that many social theorists have viewed 'marginal men' as the key figures in the study of cultural change, because of their important part in entrepreneurial and innovating activity. Some have seen them as a product of the great breaking up and mixing of cultures attendant upon migration. 'Marginal man' was 'emancipated' – freed from customary expectations – by travel and migration. Although some emigrants may want to merge into their new society, there are many who are exemplars of emancipation. Such a person, Mageean suggests, is eager for new things, explores, and partakes in the cultural life of two distinct peoples, never quite willing to break with the past even if permitted to do so, and not quite accepted in the new society because of racial or religious prejudice. Mageean argues that the idealized 'marginal men' are uniquely placed to exploit their position. Not completely part of the society of their adoption, they are free of the restrictions imposed by its value system; often too, having left their own society, they are no longer constrained by its dominant values. 'Marginal men' don't have to be migrants or belong to particular racial groups who are marginal by virtue of their ambiguous position in the society of their adoption. It is also possible for individuals to be estranged from their own society because of their own religious, political or other views.

Mageean points to examples where religious nonconformists have found themselves in the position of 'marginal men'. In the last half of the eighteenth century, such nonconformists formed only about 7 per cent of the population of England and Wales, while Scottish dissenters from the established Presbyterian church formed no higher percentage of the population of Scotland. However, these tiny groups provided half of the innovating entrepreneurs in Britain in the eighteenth and early nineteenth centuries. In proportion, these dissenting groups provided more than ten times as many innovators as did the rest of the society.

The hypothesis is that underprivilege combined with the possession of, and belief in, different value systems from that of the mainstream of society, will contribute to the development of unconventional patterns of behaviour, and a predisposition towards entrepreneurship. Historically, there are many examples of people who don't 'fit in': 'marginal men', acting in the role of entrepreneurs and innovators. Relatively unrestricted by social norms, they do not run the risk of 'social loss', and some gain the benefits of 'stranger value'. One typical example described by Bradley (1987) would be Andrew Carnegie (1835–1919). The Carnegie family was forced by economic hardship to emigrate from the UK to the USA. Andrew started work at the age of 13 for $1.40 a week as a bobbin boy in a cotton factory in Pittsburgh, Pennsylvania and went on to build the largest iron and steel works in the USA, selling out in 1901 for $480 million, making him the richest man in the world.

Further support for the 'marginal man' hypothesis comes from Shapero (1975), who argues along similar lines when talking about 'displaced persons':

> The simplest route [to becoming an entrepreneur] is falling on hard times. Most entrepreneurs are D.P's, displaced persons who have been dislodged from some nice, familiar niche, and tilted off course . . . . It also helps to be Jewish – or Palestinian, a Lebanese, an Ibo in Nigeria, a Parsi in India, a Chinese on the West Coast. It is no accident that these groups maintain their entrepreneurial traditions, they provide plenty of role models . . . . It also seems true that groups that are 'protected' or made to feel dependent, as blacks and women have been, do not produce their quota of entrepreneurs.

We examined marginalization by looking at our respondents' childhood and early life experience. Marginalization, generally, was found to be almost exclusively the province of entrepreneurs. In 47 per cent of our entrepreneurs' case studies, interviewees felt that they suffered some form of marginalization or scapegoating, either through belonging to an out-group or coming from an impoverished background, and that marginalization was in part responsible for them becoming entrepreneurs. We have selected some of the more powerful examples which show rather convincingly the effects of social, religious and physical marginalization.

Social marginalization

Peter de Savary can probably be seen as one of Mageean's archetypical 'marginal men', someone who didn't 'fit in', as an immigrant in Canada. De Savary had left England dreaming of adventure and, like the adventurers of his dreams, he was not coming back until he had proved himself, to himself and the world. He was: 'determined to show anybody that had to be shown that I could "make it"'.

During our interview, he recalled suffering the effects of marginalization as a young man. He was unskilled and, as such, unable to secure a job. Canada in the early 1960s was not known for being a welfare state. Because of its climatic conditions, it suffers from the 'boom or bust' frontier syndrome, where many jobs are seasonal. Some immigrants were looked upon by the indigenous population as taking the scarce jobs of the Canadians, and were openly referred to as DPs (displaced persons).

Out of a job, hungry and without prospects, de Savary was rather like one of Shapero's DPs. At 16, in a relatively hostile environment and without a skill, he felt it necessary to try even harder than most, as the consequences of failure would be catastrophic. Being an immigrant, he needed to construct a new self-identity. One means of doing this was to establish a business. This he did. De Savary took up babysitting, gardening and house cleaning – just about anything that would earn him a bare living. He became skilled in household servicing, and so shaped his new career.

As we noted earlier, marginality is considered an important contributing factor in the explanation of entrepreneurship in emigrants, and de Savary's case is very similar to that of the other six emigrants in our study. David Jones, Chief Executive of Grattan PLC, described an event that occurred during his youth, in a mock election in his public school. Jones was a 'free' pupil, which he saw as a stigma, and it was his introduction to social marginalization. He tried to rebel against this by leading the 'Labour' opposition in the school debate. But he was quickly 'put down' by the 'leader' of the 'Tory Party', who Jones describes as his, 'class enemy . . . and who was an absolute snob'. His opponent declared, 'You don't want to vote Labour, they eat their peas with their knives.' This remark was designed to hurt Jones, not to further the debate. All knew that Jones's mother picked peas to supplement the family income and to pay for his school uniform.

Religious marginalization

Godfrey Bradman, a philanthropist and one of Britain's leading property developers, was the person who underwrote £5 million to help the Opren sufferers fight their court case against Lilly, the manufacturer of the drug. A High Court judge, at the time, described Bradman as a fairy godparent.

As a boy Bradman lived with his parents in Long Melford, a village in Suffolk. This was during the war years (1939–45) and Bradman's father, an aircraftman in the RAF, was away from home for long periods. The family was extremely poor and lived in the bottom half of a house in the village, where the rent was ninepence (3.75p) a week.

There was nothing unusual in eking out a living during the Second World War, and not having a shilling for the electric meter cannot be thought of as a dramatic experience, but it is interesting that Bradman still recalls the experience after 50 years. However, what was unusual was the treatment the child received in the village. Being the only Jewish boy in his school, Bradman was scapegoated. Prejudice against 'out-groups' is a sad but recurring fact of social life, and Bradman learned this the hard way: 'I was beaten up most days on the way to school,' he recalls. But regardless of the beatings, Bradman was steadfast in his faith: 'I never pretended I wasn't a Jew'.

Scapegoating, marginalization and a feeling of deprivation were the prime movers that set Bradman on the entrepreneurial path:

I've always wanted to be financially secure, and I think that that was born out of deprivation . . . . I saw money as being a way of buying myself out of a constant state of penury . . . . Through an impoverished background I decided that the only way to escape was to create wealth.

England was not the only country to suffer racial prejudice. One American respondent recounts that it was not until the 1960s that the barriers of prejudice slowly began to crumble in the USA. He goes on to say that at the turn of the century, when the full flood of migration to the US was taking place, the immigrant Jew, for instance, would never have been considered remotely acceptable for posts of prestige or in public life.

Some forward thinkers may see these marginalizing barriers as breaking down in the US, whereas those looking back often see American Jews as remaining 'uneasy aliens' on the fringe of the national culture. What we see from the answers to our questions is that, in spite of their economic power, some members of minority groups still feel marginalized or unaccepted by the elite group in the society in which they operate. This point is made clear when Sir Mark Weinberg, a Jewish immigrant to Britain, and founder of Abbey Life, states: 'there is in my people . . . a desire for increased social acceptability', and 'a strong philanthropic tradition . . . combined with what is a state of insecurity, status and position . . . it's recognition in their own community [that they want] . . . if you like, they want recognition in the establishment of which they are [he is] not part'.

With the exception of Sir Mark Weinberg, our examples of marginalization so far have all been viewed as instances of what Shapero (1975) calls 'negative displacement'. But this is not the only perspective. 'Positive displacement' and physical marginalization can be other routes to entrepreneurship.

Physical marginalization

In a study of small businessmen (small of stature) in the UK, Stanworth and Curran (1973) suggested that very often the owner-manager of a business was a marginal person. By marginality they meant discontinuity between the individual's personal attributes – for example physical characteristics, intellectual make-up, social behaviour patterns – and the role or roles which he/she held in society. The adoption of the role of entrepreneur was, according to them, a behavioural response to a perceived marginal situation.

George Davies, instrumental in creating the high street chain NEXT, suffered both physical and social marginalization. During the interview we found him reliving his feeling of physical marginalization as a youth:

> It was probably the move to Crosby. Now, it's not often I tell anyone this, and it will probably bowl you over, but it's probably also my height. When I was a young lad, I was always short, I'm now about 5 feet 7 inches, when I was at school I was short and all the big guys were getting all the 'birds' . . . it wasn't easy. Then again, to grow up good looking, six foot and have everything must be the worst sort of recipe for success because you don't have to try, and life is about trying and strangely enough, some sort of affliction, providing it's not too serious, must help. It made me fight harder. When I was about 15, I was about five foot nothing, but I always had a big pal because we got on, and he, of course, would walk in [to the dance] and they would all look at him, and he would pull all the 'birds', and I would go home to Mum. It was strange you see but then I broke through.

A second significant trauma for Davies also came about when the family moved house from the relatively poor socio-economic district of Bootle to the more affluent middle-class and residential area of Crosby:

> when we moved to Crosby, most of my friends went to public school and I think that most of the mothers thought I wasn't as good as them. In a subtle way, they treated me as if I was black . . . so I understand how blacks feel, you can get very bitter or you say 'well, I'll show them!'

For Davies, the founding of his first business, School-Care Ltd, may have been an attempt to resolve the conflict resulting from marginality, although he remained socially marginalized not only by reason of his independent career but also because he felt that he did not 'fit in'. According to Bruce (1976, pp. 48–9), the marginal individual realizes that he does not 'fit'. He is, for this reason, unsure of his social role: his points of reference are in disarray and, like Peter de Savary earlier, he needs to construct a self-identity, and 'One means of finding himself is through establishing a business'(Bruce, 1976).

To this day, the rejection experienced by Davies from the 'Crosby mothers' still smarts, and he still feels that he 'must show them!' As Gilder (1986) points out,

> They are not always kind or temperate, rarely elegant or tall, only occasionally glib or manifest leaders of men. By fleeing their homes and families . . . many inflict and suffer a trauma of loss – and fight to justify and overcome it. As immigrants, many deliberately seek an orphan's fate, and toil to launch a dynasty. Many lose their fathers, early fill their role, and transcend it gloriously in the world. Ugly, they wreak beauty; rude and ruthless, they redeem the good and true. Mostly outcasts, exiles, mother's boys, rejects, warriors, they learn early the lessons of life, the knowledge of pain, the ecstasy of struggle.

It must be understood that not all marginalized individuals become entrepreneurs; this may be the only one way in which the individual can come to terms with the state of social marginality. Nor does it mean that every entrepreneur is or was marginalized. Fifty-three per cent of our entrepreneurs enjoyed perfectly normal lives, as Archer, Woolf, Berry, d'Abo, Broackes, Gummer, Flowers, Kiam II, Gorman and Campbell would attest.

SOCIAL STATUS AND STRATIFICATION

We have seen that religious, physical and cultural marginalizing influences, some researchers believe, mould individuals to become entrepreneurial. However, we might progress to a deeper understanding of entrepreneurial activity by examining the totality of relationships of the society in which they act: their social and cultural milieu.

In searching for corroborating evidence for the data collected in our sample, we can turn to George Homans. The theory espoused by Homans (1968) is directed towards explaining and predicting different responses by individuals to opportunities for economic innovation and stresses that no single variable, even ones as important as power, rank or status, is sufficient as a complete explanation, though some are rated as more important than others.

For the purpose of his research on the effect of status on behaviour, Homans used a simple classification in which individuals could occupy three different types of social position: upper, middle or lower status. He made it clearly understood that no society possesses just three levels of status, and he did not claim that any individual member can always be assigned unambiguously to one of the levels.

Homans's conclusions are derived mainly from field and experimental research work carried out by others into small groups (Kelly and Shapiro, 1954; Hughes, 1946; Blau, 1955; Asch, 1953) and, as he himself points out, we cannot generalize from the small group to society at large, although we may find that similarities exist. What his findings do demonstrate is that where differences in status between members become recognized and established, then these differences tend to stimulate further differences in their behaviour – the self-perpetuating nature of ostracization and nonconformist behaviour would be typical examples.

In his book *Social Behaviour*, Homans (1968) concludes, after reviewing the experimental research on the relationship between status and conformity, 'that it is not only members of low status, with little to lose, who are prone to nonconformity'. He argues that 'the man of high status, whose social position is secure, has also little to gain from a rigid compliance with the standards of society, and can afford to risk some loss of status'.

Concerning the man of high and established status who enjoys a margin of freedom from group control, Homans argues that, although such a man must provide rare and valuable services to others to keep his high status, as long as he does just that, other members will allow him some leeway in lesser things. This he may or may not take. If he rigorously abides by any and every norm, he may put himself back among the masses instead of keeping himself set apart. He is likely to be a leader and in a position of authority, so if there is any correcting to be done, he is the one to do it: it is his business to correct others, not others' to correct him. Therefore, if he violates group norms in small matters, it would be presumptuous of other members to tell him he is wrong.

Homans refers to violating group norms in small matters. But recently we have seen that in some instances it seems presumptuous of others to object even in the largest of matters. A typical example would be Robert Maxwell, whose financial controllers, together with independent pension watchdog bodies, did not dare to question his authority and his handling of the group's pension fund prior to his death and its investigation by the Serious Fraud Office. What is even more alarming is that one would not expect journalists to allow any violations of group norms, especially by entrepreneurs, as 'entrepreneur thrashing' (Silver, 1986, p. 40) is a favourite pastime of journalists, yet all the *Mirror's* investigative journalists, who in the past had investigated the 'great and the good', were reduced to complete impotence when they came to investigating their own 'house'. However, we have seen in this study that some people with high status, if they violate group norms to an unacceptable level, suffer ostracism – at least for a period. A typical example is Gerald Ronson and his part in the Guinness Affair.

At the other end of the scale, if we look at the possible strategy for the man (used generically) of low status and/or esteem, Homans argues that if he conforms to the group's judgement, and the group is correct, he does not get very far; one example of 'good behaviour' alone is not sufficient to elevate him. Likewise, he stands to gain nothing if he conforms and the group's judgement turns out to be incorrect. However, nonconformity can have two possible outcomes. If he rejects the group's judgement and the group is correct, he has nothing to lose because he is at the bottom anyhow. If, on the other hand, he rejects the group's judgement and the group turns out to be wrong, he turns out to be right and has something to gain. He has saved his self-respect and has been justified in doing it.

The question of respect is particularly important where low status and ostracization go hand in hand. For to ostracize someone is to remove them from social control – if the person resists conformity there is little that can be done against him as the group has lost its leverage on his behaviour; he has nothing to lose by nonconformity. Such behaviour is self-perpetuating. We see then that, according to Homans's argument, the upper-status man has little to gain by conformity, and the lower-status one little to lose by nonconformity. So, for different reasons, the behaviour of both groups tends towards nonconformity. But a member of the middle status, group stands to gain by conformity and lose by nonconformity. Those of middle-status we can argue, are less secure and can least afford a loss in status. The man in the middle's strategy of behaviour, therefore, is typically one of conformity. Homans's view of nonconformists as potential innovators is shared by Robert Bruce's (1976) 'marginal man'. Here the innovator and entrepreneur is seen as a 'deviant', that is, as one who breaks with the norm of group behaviour and goes his own way. Especially under conditions of change and novelty, it is such deviants who will follow their own judgement and take a new course of action and/or adopt a new procedure or product. Homans's theory then, can be seen as one step beyond this approach, in so far as it attempts to establish which people are best positioned strategically to take the new course without potential damaging loss.

Again, Homans's work reinforces Max Weber's theory and has helped us to hypothesize which socio-economic group generates the leaders of commerce and industry. It reveals that elite entrepreneurs in general originally come from the lower socio-economic classes as opposed to elite intrapreneurs, who are generally drawn from the upper-middle-class groups. According to this theory, middle managers would be drawn from the middle classes, and generally remain managers.

Can we use Homans's theory to throw some light on our study? We feel we can. Applying the theory to our sample, the persons of high status – Lord McAlpine, Sir Antony Pilkington, Julian Smith and others – whose social position is relatively secure, have little to gain from rigid compliance with the standards of society and can afford to risk some loss of status. This, we can argue, allows companies run by these individuals to become more entrepreneurial. If one of high status takes a commercial risk and it succeeds, the status of the intrapreneur and his firm is enhanced. If it fails, he can still maintain his status by virtue of his 'high position' in society.

The individuals of low status – those who have come from deprived backgrounds – have little to gain by respectability and nothing to lose by its opposite, thus allowing them to take greater risks whereby some might become entrepreneurs. It is the people in the middle (the managers highlighted by Clements and Norburn in the first paragraph of this chapter), especially those who see some chance of rising in the world, who seek, 'by close adherence to a rigid morality, to differentiate themselves from what they call the rabble and thereby establish their claims to social recognition' (Homans, 1968). This may well point to why many middle managers

---

Harold Woolf on marginalization:

I came on that idea a long time ago when I was in my twenties, which I thought fitted a lot of people. It ran something along these lines: the reasonable man adapts himself to the world and the unreasonable man adapts the world to himself, therefore all progress depends upon the unreasonable man.

appear risk averse and remain middle managers, thus not risking the move away from a familiar environment.

EXECUTIVE SUMMARY

Our study shows that you can still 'make it' financially, regardless of lowly origins. Seventy-two per cent of the entrepreneurs in our study were discovered to come from working-class backgrounds where their fathers worked as coal miners, plumbers, bookmakers, or clerks from the ranks in the military. Only 20 per cent of intrapreneurs were seen to have working-class origins. Marginalization was also almost exclusively the domain of the entrepreneur. Forty-seven per cent of entrepreneurs had suffered some form of marginalization, either social, physical or religious, whereas only 14 per cent of intrapreneurial interviewees came from marginal back- grounds.

Paradoxically enough, regardless of lowly origins or marginalization, and in spite of barriers or hardships, it appears that familiarity with obstacles that have to be overcome in some way has a motivating quality to the entrepreneur, driving him/her on to ever greater achievements.

5 Education

Bruce (1976) suggests that the influence of education on the career of any individual is not simply confined to technical understanding. The longer he/she stays in the educational system, the more adept does the student become at dealing with a wide variety of situations likely to arise throughout life. Through education, the individual also develops competence in the nuances and subtleties, which makes for acceptability in a certain social environment. The person who has not been through this educational process has to learn from 'experience of life'. Bruce goes on to argue that although parents have some influence in this educational process, many will not be able to arrange opportunities in a business environment nor will they have the finances to launch their offspring in a business career, on their own account. As C. Wright Mills, the eminent sociologist, once put it, 'the best statistical chance of becoming a member of the elite is to be born into it' (1956). If Bruce is correct, education and background are important in the development of both independent entrepreneurs and intrapreneurs or corporate executives.

FORMAL EDUCATION

Komives (1972) found that entrepreneurs have effectively the same level of education as the rest of the population, although 65 per cent of them drop out of school or leave early because they are bored. Cox and Cooper (1988), in a study of 45 British CEOs, found that less than half the group (18 in all) had university degrees. Two of these also had PhDs and two others had other postgraduate qualifications. Three had started university courses, but not completed them. The remaining 24 had all left school between the ages of 14 and 16. Those who did not go into higher education took up apprenticeships or entered professional offices and continued their education through evening classes. Six of the chief executives interviewed had no formal qualifications.

The education level in the Cox and Cooper study is lower than reported elsewhere. For example, Margerison (1980) found that 65 per cent of British managers had at least a first degree. The *Wall Street Journal* (cited in White, 1989) reports even high levels of education achieved among American managers: 6 per cent high school, 40 per cent university graduates, 35 per cent Master's and 13 per cent doctorates. The seemingly disparate results of these studies may be explained in terms of the different methodology used to obtain the information. Margerison and the *Wall Street Journal* studies both used postal questionnaires, from which one might expect a different response rate (i.e. the more highly qualified are more likely to respond due to their feeling of esteem).

Cox and Cooper suggest that the low level of qualifications among British CEOs may be exaggerated by the age of the sample interviewed for their study, most of whom were in their fifties. It is thought that the next generation of managers will show a higher proportion of graduates, as the trend into higher education increases.

Finally, Max Weber (1958) describes the people who demonstrate the spirit of capitalism and economic enterprise as mainly self-made men: the upwardly mobile lower-middle classes. This is supported by Ian Campbell Bradley (1987), who, when discussing 'historical entrepreneurs', suggests that it was something other than education that was responsible for entrepreneurial activity.

Our research (Table 5.1) has shown that education is not necessarily a prerequisite for success in male entrepreneurship, although the female business leaders had in general been through higher education. There is also a significant difference between the types of education received between entrepreneurs and intrapreneurs. Our data provides limited support for the suggestion that entrepreneurial activity is dominated by people with little formal education. The most striking difference is that 68 per cent of intrapreneurs were university graduates compared with only 21 per cent of entrepreneurs. Sixty-three per cent of the entrepreneurs did not even attain the grammar school level of education.

If we look at both intrapreneurs and entrepreneurs as business leaders, then we can say that the majority (68 per cent) of intrapreneurs, having been through the education system and absorbed the values it imparted, have opted for a career in a corporate life rather than striking out on the more risky road of independent entrepreneurship.

The following examples demonstrate two very different educational paths between entrepreneurs and intrapreneurs found in our research.

Owen Oyston, although rarely at school because of illness, left when he was 16. When attending school he was scapegoated by pupils because he lagged behind others in his group. Nor were his tutors any help in assisting

Table 5.1 Educational level – entrepreneurs v. intrapreneurs

Level	Percentage of entrepreneurs	Percentage of intrapreneurs	Total
Number	19	22	41
No grammar school	63%	9%	
Some grammar school	11%	9%	
Some college/university	5%	14%	
Graduate	21%	68%	

Oyston to catch up with his group, using corporal punishment in an attempt to motivate him: 'I was beaten up by the Christian Brothers . . . at the Catholic college'. Sir Nigel Broackes, founder of Trafalgar House and now its honorary president, states that he left school at 16, but it did not prevent him from becoming chairman of his own company.

A newspaper report in the *Liverpool Echo* on 19 October 1992 seems to endorse our findings on many entrepreneurs' educational path, with a story of 'millionaire, 34-year-old Frank Woodward, who left school without any qualifications and was told he was going nowhere by his teachers. Frank Woodward now has a Rolls Royce lifestyle running one of Liverpool's fastest growing companies, S & W Products Ltd.'

The intrapreneurs' schooldays and career paths were markedly different. Emma Nicholson, MP, describes her education thus: 'I went to a girls-only boarding preschool in Sussex. Then another boarding school run by Church of England nuns in Berkshire, nearer to our home. Then I went to the Royal Academy of Music.'

Similarly, we follow some male intrapreneurs as they describe their educational paths:

First I was at Codhill, a private school, after that Eton and then two years in the Life Guards, in the Household Cavalry. Then a year in France and one in Germany learning French and German. Then Oxford for three years and two years at the Harvard Business School.

Solid educational backgrounds were not restricted to British intrapreneurs. Prestigious school backgrounds were equally typical among American intrapreneurs with one American intrapreneur describing his educational background thus: 'Educated at the influential Horace Mann private school in New York, later attended Yale, the Sorbonne and Syracuse universities.'

Whatever the educational path followed, it seems not to have prevented the determined individual from achieving his/her own goals. While it might

George Davies on education:

I went to Bootle Grammar School, then I was brought up in Netherton. Looking back I'd say this: I was very good at sport. What I'm trying to describe is that you need, at school, to perhaps do well at something. It doesn't really matter whether it's maths or . . . I managed to play for England's Schoolboys (soccer) and got a trial for Liverpool, but then I decided to go to university . . . . So getting back to it. What you have to get into you somewhere is the sense of trying to get into the – first team. So if it's sport, you try to achieve something and it's the same in business. I don't personally think that there are high academic qualifications required to do well in most walks of life. Maybe to be a nuclear physicist or a computer genius . . . but in any case, most of those people cannot mix with other people.

David Jones, chief executive of NEXT PLC, on his education and career:

I set out in life to achieve something, but not knowing what I was going to achieve. I left school with three very poor A levels and didn't know what I was going to do. The Youth Employment Officer in Worcester said to me, 'Haven't you got a clue what you are going to do?' And I said, 'No, I haven't.' He said, 'For Christ's sake go and get yourself a job somewhere, and when you make up your mind what you want to do let me know.' I said, 'Fine, what should I do?' He said, 'Go and work at Kay's Mail Order Company, they are always looking for people.'

I went to Kay's and I had a very lowly job as a clerk, writing out records and such. Then I suddenly started thinking to myself, I was responsible for about 125 people who that week had sent me £500. Then I multiplied it up and thought: Crikey, this business must have received something like £75,000 that week. Now £75,000 to me was like winning the pools, I couldn't imagine £75,000. I then thought: I can get very interested in this business. So how can I make something of myself?

have served to keep the intrapreneur at the top, for the entrepreneur it was just another hill to climb in overcoming adversity, and may even have acted as an additional spur. What our investigation into educational backgrounds indicates is that there is a contrast between the relatively high risk-averse professional business manager or intrapreneur, and the flair and innovativeness of the relatively less educated and risk-seeking entrepreneur. It is interesting to speculate that these relatively untrained entrepreneurs, lacking in large part the necessary formal or professional management training and qualifications, but who have created vast business empires, might have found it extremely difficult to get a job in these same organizations had they been created by others! Would any personnel manager have considered employing Richard Branson if he had applied for a management job in Virgin Airways, had it been owned by, say, British Airways?

MANAGEMENT EDUCATION

Ronnie Lessem (1987) has argued that until the 1950s, at least in Great Britain, management was not a subject that was formally taught. The Victorian entrepreneurs, who were in the vanguard of the Industrial Revolution, were essentially self-made men growing up in the 'hard school of life'. As Ian Campbell Bradley (1987) reports, they had acquired their knowledge through personal experience, finding their own methods of mastering both business and engineering. In contrast, Lessem argues that the business and management schools that later grew up on both sides of the Atlantic appear to have adopted a highly impersonal approach. The fear, for Lessem, seems to be that academia is breeding an elite group of business 'analysts', removed from the more personal qualities possessed by earlier business leaders and entrepreneurs. As Lessem argues, it may well be that the business schools have been producing masters of business *administration* rather than masters of *business*. It is interesting that, as Naisbitt (1984) has pointed out, two of the most successful post-Second World War industrial nations, Japan and West Germany, are noted for their lack of business schools.

Support for Lessem's argument comes from McCall, Lombardo and Morrison (1988), who have shown how executives learn from assignments:

> In general, adults learn when they need to or have to, and these executives were no exception . . . . Because of the demanding nature of these assignments, learning was not a nicety – something to be done out of interest or because it might be helpful. Learning was something these managers did because they had little choice but to take action – stab at

problems even if they weren't sure what they were doing, because doing nothing was surely unacceptable.

Charles Handy (1976) also found that British managers received far less business education than managers in other countries. On the basis of this finding, Handy suggests that 'management in Britain has traditionally been more to do with pragmatism than professionalism'. Other studies have supported the suggestion that management development is a matter of experience and not academia (Mumford, 1985).

Our results suggest that to follow a 'linear' intrapreneurial path in some major corporation and hope to rise to lead that corporation, education and management training is of considerable value. Academia has been one aspect of training intrapreneurs for their positions. Fifteen of the 21 intrapreneurs who answered questions on education had received university training as economists (3), lawyers (2), engineers (4) and accountants (6). Eight of the 15 had also attended some type of business school for at least one year, which helped to groom them for leadership in the organization.

To follow the more turbulent entrepreneurial path, formal training has not been seen as an absolute necessity. Of the entrepreneurs in our study, three became accountants after studying in adult educational evening classes, two served apprenticeships as solicitors and four were university trained. The remaining ten entrepreneurs had relatively little formal training to become business leaders and followed 'spiral' career paths moving from firm to firm to gain knowledge before applying the springboard tactic of branching out on their own. Like those who embodied Weber's 'spirit of capitalism', they were: 'as a rule . . . neither dare-devil adventurers . . . nor simply great financiers . . . on the contrary, they were the men who had grown up in the hard school of life' (Weber, 1958).

We do not, of course, argue that entrepreneurs in some way do not need to be educated or that a lack of education is beneficial to entrepreneurial activity. Entrepreneurs, it appears, learn from 'hands-on' experience which is necessary in order to succeed, and having that learning reinforced by success makes a potent teacher. Even so, we found that some entrepreneurs understood the benefits of education, and later in their careers continued their education at night school or in part-time courses.

'Never stop learning' seems to be almost automatic for any type of successful business leader. John Kotter (1982), for example, observed that 'the most effective GMs [general managers] had careers characterized by almost constant growth in their knowledge of the business and organization, and in their relationship with relevant others'.

Bennis and Nanus (1985), in their study of 90 top leaders, documented the same kind of thing: 'Nearly all leaders are highly proficient in learning from experience. Most were able to identify a small number of mentors and key experiences that powerfully shaped their philosophies, personalities, aspirations and operating styles. And all of them regard themselves as "stretching", "growing", and "breaking new ground".'

'GUARDIAN ANGELS'

Since there is no school for successful entrepreneurs and they do not have formal training in entrepreneurship, their skills must be acquired elsewhere. We wanted to find out what help, if any, entrepreneurs and intrapreneurs receive from others while following the path to success. Consequently we asked if they could identify people who had acted as 'mentors' or 'guardian angels' during their career. The entrepreneurs were rarely able to identify such an individual. In fact only two admitted that they were not entirely and solely responsible for their own success: they see themselves as self-made. Intrapreneurs admitted to having much more support from others. Analysis of our data from the interviews revealed that statistically intrapreneurs were much more likely to have had the support of others than were entrepreneurs. It follows that entrepreneurs, being 'lone wolves', would have had less exposure to mentors or 'guardian angels' than those who climb the corporate ladder of success. For example, when asked if he had a guardian angel, Eddy Shah replied:

> No, I was pretty much a loner, I would not have sold my house to go into printing if there were any guardian angels about. One of the problems that entrepreneurs have . . . is that very rarely do they have any formal training because they learn as they go along. What I didn't have was experience in dealing with Fleet Street cabals.

Victor Kiam II, the American entrepreneur, agrees: 'I had no "guardian angel", but I did have a coterie of very bright and able people to whom I could turn for suggestions and advice.' Although Kiam did not have a 'guardian angel', he did have a mentor.

> I believe that the former president of International Latex Corporation, with whom I worked some twenty years, was the stimulation for my basic drive and also set down the guidelines, many of which I have followed in the direction and growth of a company.

Some respondents acknowledged help and advice from others and indicated people who had helped them to get started in business, but still could not identify one predominant mentor and guide. For example, Peter de Savary could not recall any specific individual:

No . . . I haven't had one specific one, although I would not have done what I have done without many, many 'guardian angels' or many helping hands along the way. But there hasn't been one specifically, that I could actually say: that man, doing what he did, really gave me a break. A lot of people have helped me over a long period and I think you need that help to the end of your days.

What you need to do is to develop a personality and a way of life that ensures from a young age until the end of your career that there are always lots of people who would like to help you on your way. I think that is what I was saying earlier: from one's own efforts and successes there is a lot of putting back into the community, in all sorts of ways, including giving opportunity to others. I mean, that's why I am the chairman of the West Country Region of the Prince's Youth Business Trust, and I have contributed a million pounds to that. Why, you might ask? Because that is a trust, and what we are doing is creating self-employed opportunities for people under 25 who must, in the first instance, be unemployed. We will lend them money and give our time and business advice, to help them start a business, whether it's window cleaning or plumbing or taxi driving, or whatever. And I think that's one of the more satisfying things.

Some interviewees who had 'guardian angels' had been noticed for having flair or skill in a specific field. Lord Young, an excellent orator, was noticed by Isaac Wolfson when he was giving a speech at a wedding reception. Wolfson realized that here was a communicator he could use. Lord Young was offered a job with the Great Universal Stores and stayed for five years, a useful period for developing his skills.

Four entrepreneurs remained with firms until their learning curve developed to a degree where they felt that they could 'make it' on their own. This path, however, was not without its problems. Those who had used other firms as a springboard for their own development sometimes suffered the wrath of the corporation. One entrepreneur was fired when he refused to give a guarantee that he would remain with the company. Another, after 11 years with one firm, was 'sacked' because of a rumour (untrue) that had circulated, intimating that he was going to start a business on his own.

Mentors or guardian angels seem to be mainly the province of the intrapreneurs. When these respondents were asked about mentors, the answer was usually 'yes', with 12 of the 19 intrapreneurs who answered this question identifying a mentor or guardian angel. The mentor often turned out to be an immediate supervisor at an early stage in the respondent's career. This was not usually a formal mentoring arrangement, but simply a good boss who had provided help and guidance.

Furthermore, the majority of intrapreneurs (13 of the 19) were all in very successful family businesses and their response to the question on mentors or guardian angels was that the family itself had provided the necessary direction. Julian Smith, a main board director of W.H. Smith explains: 'Well . . . not really, but I suppose the family acts as the guardian angel to each of us.'

This was a common response by other intrapreneurs. Norman Burrough of Beefeater Gin recounts simply that, 'a "guardian angel" was not necessary. I got all the help I needed from within the family business.' And Sir Adrian Cadbury says, 'I was very much helped by a cousin, who was my predecessor as chairman; although he had a son of his own in the firm, he influenced my choice as his successor.' The late Lord McAlpine of Moffat replied along similar lines: 'McAlpine's was a family business . . . my father was, however, influential in guiding me'.

There was, however, the occasional exception. Jennifer d'Abo, an extremely successful entrepreneur, describes her 'guardian angel' as follows:

Oh yes, there's mine [*pointing to a photograph of Lionel Green, the father of the former Director of Public Prosecution*]. I loved that man more than anyone else in the world; he invented me. He was a great entrepreneur in his own right. He was the kindest, most generous giver. I met him when I was about 21. When I went into business he gave me my trade references. He had to make them up as we went along because I didn't have any. Whenever I needed advice, or whenever I was going to do something dotty, like buying a bankrupt department store, Lionel would say; 'Oh wonderful darling, wonderful, what a good idea. Come over and talk to me about it.' Then he would have a whole list of names of people to give me for advice. He was a star.

Martin Laing, who one would expect to have had a mentor or 'guardian angel', being the boss of a fourth-generation family firm, didn't have one:

I haven't got one . . . you see when you are at the top there are very few people you can go and chat to. God knows who Mrs Thatcher talks to confidentially. Y'know what I mean . . . you've got to have somebody, so you've got your wife; that's fine on the emotional side, but on the business side if you've got to do something? Should you do this, or do that?

To come back to the question of a mentor, I suppose my uncle is the nearest one I've got. Often I discuss things with him but surprisingly nothing is new. Businesses go in cycles and what is different is timing.

So an idea that he had wouldn't work then, but now it would work because the environments are different. What I haven't yet done, and I said that I would do is, I must go down to the Patent Office for the 1800s–1900s and see the number of inventions that didn't actually come to anything. The time might be right for them now, actually.

David Jones was extremely forthright in identifying his guardian angel:

My benefactor, in my early years, was definitely David Wolfson. He was the guy that recognized my potential and promoted me in my early years. I had lunch with him yesterday. I still remember the things he said to me. 'Don't sit back and wait for things to happen, get off your arse and make them happen.' Yes, I think David Wolfson was the guy who picked me, and he was the guy that probably taught me more than anyone else.

Allowing for the odd exception, it can be seen that the responses from each group are quite different. The elite independent entrepreneurs do not, in general, see themselves as having any sort of 'guardian angel'. Following a more spiral career path, they would have had little opportunity for working with individuals likely to be seen as mentors. They understand well that initial phase which many entrepreneurs must pass through before achieving their goal: 'the purgatory of entrepreneurship'.

Elite intrapreneurs, mainly having been born into the family owning the company, did not need them. Intrapreneurs continuing the family business see their families as providing all the support they needed. The remainder of intrapreneurs, by virtue of working their way up within an organization, are most likely to receive advice and guidance from certain senior or 'significant others'. This, quite simply, reflects their different situations.

EXECUTIVE SUMMARY

An education which qualifies the individual for economics, engineering or accounting seems to be the preferred option for the intrapreneurs. Entrepreneurs have come from a variety of educational backgrounds but, again, accountancy is popular, although they are much less likely than intrapreneurs to have a university degree. Sixty-eight per cent of intrapreneurs graduated from university, whereas only 21 per cent of entrepreneurs achieved a university degree. A university or business school education is not a prerequisite to success as an entrepreneurial business leader. However, if you want to climb to the top of the corporate ladder within a large organization, or assume the leadership of a family firm, it is best to have a university degree and some business school experience. Intrapreneurs are far more likely than entrepreneurs to have had a mentor or guardian angel who helped and supported them during the early stages of their career.

6　The work ethic

William Whyte (1956), in *The Organization Man*, describes how De Tocqueville made a prophecy. If America ever destroyed its genius it would be by intensifying the social virtues at the expense of other virtues, by making the individual come to regard himself as hostage to prevailing opinion; by creating, in sum, a tyranny of the majority. Whyte argues that this is what the 'Organization Man' is doing; that society through its culture and circumstances has evolved a certain type of modal personality. By 'Organization Man', Whyte means the 'faceless' leaders and bureaucrats of American big business and institutions. Whyte goes on to say that the 'Organization Man' sincerely believes in what he is doing, but this conviction only makes the tyranny more powerful. At the very time when the pressures of our highly organized society make so stringent a demand on the individual, he is not only 'other-directed' (unduly influenced by outside forces), to borrow Riesman's (1950) concept, he is putting forth a philosophy which tells him this is the *right* path to follow.

Whyte argues that, officially, Americans hold to the Protestant Ethic. However, because of the narrow and restrictive implications of the term, many would deny its relevance to them; but let them expound the 'American Dream', and they virtually define the Protestant Ethic. This same ethic, it can be argued, was rekindled in Britain with the coming of Thatcher's 'Enterprise Culture'.

A study by Birch and his associates at MIT (reported in Gilder, 1986) provides data which reinforces Whyte's belief that the independent entrepreneur is not dead. Birch conducted a comprehensive analysis of the facts of small (American) businesses. Using records of 5.6 million firms from Dun and Bradstreet, Birch reached the conclusion that companies with fewer than a hundred employees created 80 per cent of the net new jobs in the US during the 1970s. Gilder goes on to say that data from the 1980s confirm Birch's findings, and adds that:

entrepreneurs, though many are not churchgoers, emerge from a culture shaped by religious values. The optimism and trust, the commitment and faith, the discipline and altruism that their lives evince and their works require, all can flourish only in the midst of a moral order, with religious foundation.'

(Gilder, 1986)

Max Weber, in *The Protestant Ethic and the Spirit of Capitalism* (1958), examined the relationship between the rise of Protestantism and the eventual development of Western industrial capitalism. He argued that capitalist enterprises are organized on rational bureaucratic lines. Business transactions are conducted in a systematic and rational manner, with costs and projected profits being carefully assessed. Underlying this 'practice' Weber found the 'spirit' of capitalism: a set of ideas, ethics and values. He illustrates this 'spirit of capitalism' by quotations from two books by Benjamin Franklin, *Necessary Hints to Those That Would be Rich* (1736) and *Advice to a Young Tradesman* (1748). Franklin, as quoted by Weber (1958), wrote:

Remember that time is money. He that can earn ten shillings a day by his labour, and goes abroad, or sits idle, one half of the day, though he spends but sixpence during his diversion or idleness, ought not to reckon that the only expense; he has really spent, or rather thrown away, five shillings besides. Time wasting, idleness and diversion lose money. Remember that credit is money. A reputation for prudence and honesty will bring credit as will paying debts on time. A businessman should behave with industry and frugality, and punctuality and justice in all his dealings.

Franklin reminded his reader that:

The most trifling actions that affect a man's credit are to be regarded. The sound of your hammer at five in the morning, or eight at night, heard by a creditor, makes him easy six months longer; but if he sees you at a billiard table, or hears your voice at a tavern, when you should be at work, he sends for his money the next day. . . . It shows, besides, that you are mindful of what you owe; it makes you appear careful as well as an honest man, and still increases your credit.

Franklin, writing in the eighteenth century, focused on several important areas, including shrewdness, calculation, deferred gratification and time itself as a measurable commodity. From our interviews, it can be seen that these same traits are still important for today's business leaders. In general our interviewees exemplify values of a kind that Weber found in the

Victor Kiam II, discussing his goals:

I have always worked for the accomplishment of goals and found that the financial rewards have come. I think the entrepreneurs who work for money alone, and have to display their wealth through materialism, such as gold chains, expensive automobiles, etc., are not the true entrepreneurs. The true entrepreneur gets a satisfaction from the sense of accomplishment, from the pride of having achieved his or her goals. The financial rewards are a by-product once one has the necessities of life.

My goal today is to build a multi-national company, a leader in its field, and one of which I can be proud. Starting ten years ago with a significant brand identity and a marvellous product, the company has been able to expand over the past decade more than ten-fold in total volume. As a private company, our company, Remington, is competing with the giants of the world, N.V. Phillips, Matsushita, etc. and we are succeeding. To me that is motivation.

extracts he cites from Franklin, and which he believed formed the intellectual and psychological basis of capitalism.

Admittedly, one of our intrapreneurs expresses some scepticism about the role of Weber's 'Protestant Ethic'. There are, he says

the elect, and God acknowledges His view of the elect by their worldly goods, which always struck me as being odd. I like the comment that you can see how little God thinks of money by the people He gives it to! . . . Although once again I may be wrong, I believe that the top people in any field are really playing a game. They want to shine for reasons of ego, for reasons of the delight in the exercise of skills, or whatever. I believe that the medals and the rewards, and in the case of businessmen the money they get, are just the markers in the game. Sir James Goldsmith in England, or Rupert Murdoch or Donald Trump or whoever, if they make another colossally successful deal tomorrow morning, they will not have two breakfasts the next day. And if their latest venture is a disappointment they will not forgo breakfast.

However, amongst the other interviewees there was a high level of agreement in the expression of values consistent with those suggested by Weber. George Davies echoes Franklin's emphasis on the importance of a reputable image and respectability: 'I've always felt that my greatest strength was my principles. I've found that it created loyalty for me . . . . Integrity [to me] means that if I say that I will do something, I'll never let anyone down. I won't wheedle out of it, if it turns bad.

This same theme is mentioned by Tony Berry. When answering a question on honesty and trust, he replied: 'you usually find that their [enterpreneurs'] word is their bond'. Later he added: 'It has always been on the basis of trust with people that I have done deals.'

Weber argued that the 'spirit of capitalism' was not simply a way of making money, but a way of life which had ethics, duties and moral obligations. We see this reflected in Gerald Ronson's attitude when he says, 'I have refused to dump my gas stations, even though they are now just marginally profitable . . . I need this business like I need a hole in the head. But what am I going to do with the employees who have been with me 25 years if I shut it down?'

Weber examines the rise of what he terms 'ascetic Protestantism', which he maintained preceded and was a precondition for the development of Western capitalism. He was concerned with the guidelines and directives for conduct laid down by his ascetic Protestantism, which certainly included the need for a 'calling' in life, a well-defined career which is pursued in a determined, single-minded manner.

Gerald Ronson gives a modern twist to what Weber termed the 'calling', and the commitment it requires from the individual: 'If you want to be really successful in business, don't think that you can play at it . . . . It does require total, single-minded dedication.' And, 'There are no short-cuts to building up a major enterprise . . . it's all about starting at the foundations.'

The modern business leaders we interviewed could clearly be seen to perpetuate some of the traits and characteristics identified by Weber as part of the make-up of the capitalist business leader. Other aspects of the 'Puritan syndrome', such as the link between industriousness, thrift, self-control and wealth accumulation, are also still relevant to modern entrepreneurs and intrapreneurs.

John Wesley, the leader of the great Methodist revival, which accompanied the expansion of English industry at the close of the eighteenth century, believed that there was a connection between religion, frugality and wealth: 'For religion must necessarily produce industry and frugality, and these cannot but produce riches. We must exhort all Christians to gain what they can and to save all they can; that is, in effect to grow rich' (quoted in Weber, 1958). In practice this meant reinvesting one's profits in the business.

The direct economic effects of a Puritan mode of life, involving work on non-religious 'holy days' (only the weekly Sabbath giving abstinence from work) were manifest in two ways. In the first instance, this type of life worked powerfully towards the limitation of consumption and, through saving, facilitated investment. Secondly, the intensified activity in one's 'calling', which Puritanism encouraged, led to vastly increased production. Moneymaking was now freed from the traditional disgrace which had been attached to it. Profits, already legalized, were now coming to be looked upon as willed by God, as a mark of His favour and a proof of the success of one's 'calling'.

The rigid limitations of consumption and the methodical intensification of production, Weber believed, could have only one result – the accumulation of capital through savings. Thus, the greatest possible productivity in work and the rejection of luxury were part of an ascetic Protestant style of life, which stressed the connection between hard work, thrift, abstinence and religious salvation. This accorded, Weber said, 'with the doctrine of predestination, where man, in his own mind and not through the agency of another being, was to understand the word of God and seek assurance as to whether or not he was "saved" '. Salvation, and thus social status, was indicated by the success of a man's industry, since worldly success, a secondary token of divine favour, might further indicate God's greater favour to an individual in vouchsafing his predestined salvation.

Protestants in search of the success that announced God's approval attacked time-wasting, laziness, idle gossip and taking more sleep than was necessary – prescribing six to eight hours a night at most; in fact, they denounced anything that might divert or distract a man from his 'calling'. Weber concluded that 'restless, continuous, systematic work in worldly calling must have been the most powerful conceivable lever for the expansion of the spirit of capitalism'.

In most modern societies the quest for some direct sign of divine approval has disappeared, but the dynamic drive that Weber found in his predestination and haunted Calvinist businessmen is still very much in evidence in today's business leaders. For example, Jones, Guthrie, Woolf, Peter de Savary, Ronson and many others we interviewed don't know how to stop working: they always seem restless, work 15–18-hour days, take few holidays, abound with energy and have considerable wealth. Ronson, we saw earlier insists that 'It requires total, single-minded dedication'. Ronson elaborates on the 'Weberian' theme of 'dedication': 'it all comes back to the fact that you have got to have that single-mindedness, be prepared to work seven days a week; you've got to be prepared to work 15 or 16 hours a day. It's that single-minded dedication, getting a formula, something you believe in, something that you saw that other people don't see.' Later he goes on 'you have to have discipline, and discipline is one of the main factors'.

David Jones is another 15-hour-a-day man. He cannot escape the workplace or thinking about the workplace:

When I give up working or thinking about work I'll die. I have always said to myself that if I come to work one Monday morning and I don't really want to come because I feel a bit jaded, I'll worry about it. If I came to work on two consecutive Monday's feeling the same way, I'll pack the job up.

Harold Woolf is another good example:

Well, I never stop thinking about it [business]. People in business on their own account don't stop thinking about it both night and day, there is no time when you can say to yourself, well I cannot think about this because I'm playing golf.

Michael Guthrie, in his 'calling', does not seek divine approval, but his dynamic drive and control during his leadership of Mecca is equal to anything that haunted Calvinist businessmen:

I get bored on holidays, and a fortnight is absolute madness. I deal in days . . . I'm very poor at doing nothing. Even when I go skiing, I suppose that every other day I will contact London just to keep in touch . . . I think we are similar to what an artist must be like on stage . . . it's the applause, I suppose. In terms of achievement, you know when you have done a good job and you know that everybody else knows you have done a good job. And if you acknowledge that other people recognize that that is a job well done, this is the equivalent of applause and that can mean an awful lot. You don't feel very good if you have not really performed very well, because you know everybody else knows that you have not performed very well. That can be very depressing but, in fact, it encourages you to do a damn sight better.

CAPITALISM AND CHRISTIANITY

Professor Brian Griffiths, according to Morris (1991), influenced much of the Thatcher government's thinking and upholds an outlook which can also be seen reflected in the answers of some interviewees. Morris quotes Griffiths as saying that he 'seeks to establish the legitimacy of business enterprise and the market economy within a Christian framework'. Griffiths contends that while materialism, injustice and greed are in fundamental conflict with Christian teaching, the creation of wealth to sustain life is not. Particular cultural values are necessary for the operation of the market, and these have been eroded in the recent past. These values are to be fostered by Christian values and virtues.

The Protestant work ethic had, of course, been freely adopted by Margaret Thatcher. This is illustrated in her statement that the 'spirit of this

Harold Woolf on the value of achievement:

I think people who are successful desire to do things better, they want to provide something in a better way than it's been done before. In a way, it may sound a bit stupid, but it's like giving. They actually want to give or provide something better, and the result of that, curiously enough, is to get something out of it. Then you talk about the need to achieve; well, I think of the kick of doing something well . . . doing a good deal . . . providing a better service, the adrenalin you get from that, I would put as a factor. It must be right. If you are walking along the street and bump into somebody you know, or you go to dinner and they know that you are successful, you must feel better than if you were walking along and you were just . . . Fred Bloggs. It's like if you walk along with a sun-tan, it makes you feel better.

nation is a Christian one': that is, in terms of its heritage of belief in the Almighty, and in tolerance, moral absolutes and the work ethic. Creating wealth, Mrs Thatcher went on, was a Christian obligation 'if we are to fulfil our role as stewards of the resources and talents the Creator has provided for us' (Morris, 1991).

Griffiths, in *Morality and the Market Place* (1982), explains that historically the values that allowed for the development of capitalism were Christian values, and only these could ensure its continuance. The greatest English analyst of a specific link between religion and the rise of capitalism was, perhaps, R.H. Tawney. According to Tawney (1987), Puritanism was the schoolmaster of the English middle classes:

> It heightened their virtues, sanctified, without eradicating, their convenient vices, and gave them an inexpugnable assurance that, behind virtues and vices alike, stood the majestic and inexorable laws of an omnipotent Providence, without whose foreknowledge not a hammer could beat upon the forge, not a figure could be added to the ledger. But it is a strange school which does not teach more than one lesson, and the social reactions of Puritanism, trenchant, permanent, and profound, are not to be summarized in the simple formula that it fostered individualism.

Earlier, Weber in his *Protestant Ethic*, had expounded the thesis that Calvinism, in its Anglo-Saxon version, was the parent of capitalism. But Tawney argued that the

> heart of man holds mysteries of contradiction which live in virogous

incompatibility together. When the shrivelled tissues lie in our hand, the spiritual bond still eludes us. In every human soul there is a socialist and an individualist, an authoritarian and a fanatic for liberty, as in each there is a Catholic and a Protestant. The same is true of the mass movements in which men marshall themselves for common action.

NON-CHRISTIAN ETHIC: EXPANDING THE FOCUS

However, Weber's emphasis on the operative role of distinctively Christian values may be exaggerated. This becomes clear when we look at those interviewees of non-Christian minorities. One Jewish interviewee discussed his business ethic, and how he interprets the 'calling' of good men: 'what is necessary is a vision and then a realistic progression of steps to achieve the vision . . . I think that that is one important component for good men.' By 'good men', this intrapreneur means men who are 'ends-orientated': the builders or creators of industry, as opposed to men who are 'means-orientated' and 'shark like', or as Tennyson put it of 'nature red in tooth and claw' – the predators in the market-place. These latter business-men have been taken to epitomize an 'amoral' capitalism, perhaps best described by Edward Heath in the 1970s, when he referred to 'the un-acceptable face of capitalism'.

Another example of an economically successful member of a minority group is Lord Young. Young is Jewish, his family settling in England at the turn of the century. He possesses an equally strong Jewish work ethic, which parallels and pre-dates Weber's Protestant ethic, and is derived from his original Jewish roots. Perhaps the ethic that became Young's most powerful motivator can best be described as a combined *Judaeo-Christian* work ethic.

Young's case also raises questions about the relationship between enterprise, social class and 'outsiders', whether of religion, race or social affiliation. Lord Young also raises interesting issues when he talks about education, cultural values and the alleged hostility of Britain's system of elite acculturation towards an enterprise culture. His reflections are useful, not only in revealing the consciousness of an entrepreneur, but in setting up an historical hypothesis about values.

Lord Young's 1985 Gresham lecture (Keat and Abercombie, 1991) developed the historical background to explain why the British should require an enterprise education. Lord Young insists that *enterprise* is a natural quality that has only to be 'set free'. Further, he insists that entre-preneurs and their enterprises are thwarted and their impact reduced by British culture, mainly by the 'gentrification process'. Young went on to claim that enterprising British capitalists had traditionally sent their children to public schools, where the teaching of science was resisted and the stress was on the classics. Industry and enterprise were seen as vulgar – what Young referred to as the 'stigma of utility' – and he quotes *Tom Brown's School Days*, in which business is described as 'mere money making'. Lord Young traced the pattern whereby the sons of entrepreneurs went on to Oxbridge, where business and enterprise were 'denounced', and contended that the British educational system inculcated cultural values that were hostile to enterprise. The family firms set up by entrepreneurs were used as 'milch-cows' for the gentrification of later generations (Keat and Abercrombie, 1991). We find support for this analysis from an American interviewee already quoted, who adds another perspective to the issue of 'gentrification', and to the analysis of what Young saw as the failure of the British educational system to sustain an entrepreneurial ethos. This intrapreneur describes his ideas on the creation of wealth, and how it can be lost through 'gentrification'.

This American's concept of entrepreneurial wealth creation indicates a relationship between the founder of the family fortune and the inheritors of that fortune: the son, the grandson and other descendants. Basically, the model is as follows: the 'hungry' founder desires wealth: perhaps he has seen, and has resented, his parents receiving crumbs from the table of 'Lady Bountiful'. The 'founder' does not care about 'form' (i.e. style, polish and refinement); his only interest is in 'substance' (money). On achieving his aim (wealth), he typically sends his son to a fee-paying school and then on to university. Gradually, the son develops an identity, not only as his father's son but in relation to 'significant others' who help shape his life. He now tends to be removed from 'substance', since a university education and other socializing events influence the 'son', so that he wants to change or modify his reference group from 'substance' to 'form'. The son has been taught early to want 'substance' (wealth), but now he wants more: he also wants 'form'. His role model changes from that of his father and his father's quest for wealth, to that of his new peer group and the elite culture to which he has been exposed in 'academia'.

In due time, the grandson comes along, but he is twice removed from the 'substance' and has no understanding of it: he knows only 'form' and social acceptance. Finally, when the great-grandsons take control of the wealth, they become vulnerable to market predators, through ignorance of 'substance'. For the great-grandson, who has always lived in style, detached from the realities of moneymaking, views this as the natural order of things, a divine right. These later generations are the groups who, 'go down in great crashes, these are the people whose assets are wiped away . . . by market predators'. Then the cycle begins again. This is very similar to what the entrepreneur John Adams said two centuries earlier, 'I work hard so that my children may study politics and their children may study art' (quoted in Silver, 1986).

BUSINESS ETHIC OF ENTREPRENEURIAL ACTIVITY

So far we have examined the value systems that historians such as Max Weber – as well as entrepreneurs and intrapreneurs including our more reflective interviewees, such as Young and Rose – suggest have played a part in the accumulation and creation of wealth as well as seeing it being wiped away. (Lord Young lost his fortune in the bank and property crash of the 1970s.) The ingredients of an 'enterprise culture' and the mind-set of business leaders are thus slowly being pieced together.

The reflections of Lord Young and of Daniel Rose on the ideological, psychological, educational and moral basis of wealth creation can now be seen against a background of analysis of values broadly in the tradition of Weber and Tawney. However, commentators such as Young and Rose attach more and more environmental attributes to an 'enterprise-friendly' culture than did Weber and Tawney, with their heavy concentration on the religious environment as facilitating or obstructing enterprise.

Lord Young's and several other interviewees' understanding of what we shall call the 'business ethic of entrepreneurial activity' can be generalized as follows:

1 All our case studies tend to see mankind in general as being or needing to be productive members of society, who interpret their life-chances other than from the perspective of a zero-sum game, that is, 'that the gains of one are the losses of the other'. They see latent entrepreneurial potential in particular as being randomly distributed throughout society and needing only to be 'set free'. The findings of our study, however, suggest that randomness has little to do with actual entrepreneurial flair.

2 Lord Young and others suggest that entrepreneurial activity is divided into two streams: 'ends-orientated' activity and 'means-orientated' activity. The 'ends-orientated' entrepreneurs are the builders, the constructors, the benefactors to society. The 'means-orientated' entrepreneurs are the market manipulators, the predators in society. One of the stated aims of Lord Young (like Prime Minister Edward Heath before him) was to curb the activities of 'means-orientated' entrepreneurs.

3 One intrapreneur sees the 'ends-orientated' entrepreneur as 'shining in use'. His traits or mind-set consist of a clear vision with the desire to 'grow to one's full height', together with the expression of capacities

Daniel Rose's view of the work ethic:

Happiness is a by-product that comes from various things, one of which is the exercise of one's vital powers along lines of excellence. And various people have felt, and I believe it to be true, that it is doing what you think is important. Doing it as well as you are able to do. So I believe that part of the human condition is that when a human being puts his head on the pillow at night, whether he has won, lost or drawn, if he can put his head on the pillow and say it was an important fight and I have given it my best, I think that makes for a kind of serenity and spiritual purity whose by-product is apt to be happiness. I think that is one important component for good men. In all fields, you also have just the sheer delight that comes from doing something well. The pride of the craftsman in his product.

and talents or his need for self-actualization. He sees the entrepreneur as having a goal and striving to move resolutely towards it. Entrepreneurs are 'ends-orientated', the 'ends' being their particular vision.

Lord Young suggests that the entrepreneur should be capable of succeeding within the existing framework of society. His entrepreneurs are high-energy types, whose 'reach must exceed their grasp'. But overlying all these traits is a spiritual and philosophical umbrella. The entrepreneur must be a productive member of society – a builder, not a manipulator. He must excel in his field, be attracted by his field, and have the characteristics to succeed in his field.

4 Lord Young suggests that an entrepreneur, whether 'means-orientated' or 'ends-orientated', cannot blossom unless the environment is capable of supporting and nurturing such an individual. Indeed, Lord Young's aim was to create such a society in Britain during his tenure.

Another interviewee argues that there are three general types of environment: stimulating, neutral and repressive. Entrepreneurs in general come to fruition in stimulating, Western-type societies. For evidence, he points to the immigrants, and in particular the Jewish immigrants, who came to the US in large numbers from the late nineteenth century onwards. He argues that marginalized Jews in other environments of tightly structured 'traditionalistic' (Weberian) societies, for example Spain, failed to 'succeed' in comparison with those in the more mobile, loosely structured society of the USA. He also cites the Asian immigrants in East Africa as being more 'successful' than their brothers at home.

5 Given a business ethic mind-set, together with a stimulating environment, the fledgling entrepreneur must be attracted by his chosen field and competent in it. He must generate within himself the 'pride of the craftsman' and the 'sheer delight that comes from doing something well'. Further, he must understand that a progression of steps is required to achieve his goal. To implement his plan, the entrepreneur must be able to communicate and have the cooperation of the other implementors of his plan; 'wish-lists' (ideas which are not based on sound economic reasoning) are for others. The vision of the entrepreneur must be 'do-able'.

6 Finally, it was suggested by one intrapreneur that initial fortuitous events or good luck must grace the entrepreneur's path. And he must realize that good luck is an opportunity for which he must be prepared.

In looking at entrepreneurs who fail to achieve their goals, we might say that the reason for failure is often that the requirements of cooperation placed on entrepreneurs by the community are not heeded. The social costs of departures or 'deviance' from the dominant value system, which often shows a more cautious approach to innovation and desire for change than the entrepreneur would like, often make the enterprise and the entrepreneur unacceptable. Rose, an interviewee who lectured in London in 1987, outlined this point, in particular when he talks of the local authority sometimes being at odds with and misunderstanding the entrepreneur's vision and role in urban development.

So we can see the parallels between much of the work of Tawney, Weber, Franklin, Wesley and Griffiths and our interviewees' own motivations. This boils down to a set of ideas, ethics, values, duties and obligations, held by people who are always restless, abounding with energy, wealthy and charitable.

What we have tried to demonstrate by examining the work of Tawney, Weber and Griffiths and the interviewees is that a common 'business ethic' applicable to non-Christian religious minorities as well as Protestants seems to generalize better to our existing multi-religious society than the narrow focus of Weber's Protestant work ethic.

EXECUTIVE SUMMARY

Almost much the same work ethic, described by Benjamin Franklin, that had a man's hammer ringing on his anvil at five in the morning or eight at night in the eighteenth century, has the workaholic business leaders of the twentieth century devoting 15 hours a day to some property deal or other business activity. The Calvinist quest for a direct sign of divine approval has disappeared. The religious 'calling' and glorification of God may not be the main motivators today, but the idea of self-sacrifice and forgoing pleasure today in the hope of reaping rewards tomorrow is still strong. Many also spoke about the need for integrity and claimed that 'their word is their bond' or, as Davies explained, 'I won't wheedle out of it if it goes bad'. The rigid limitations of consumption connecting frugality and wealth no longer exist. Few, if any, of our sample lived frugally, and there is evidence of conspicuous consumption by many.

Weber's Protestant work ethic, has in part, been replaced by a simple work ethic, and in the modern world of bureaucracy and the 'Organization Man' there is ample evidence that there is still room for the entrepreneur. 'Good men', ends-orientated builders of industry are how some see themselves. But the market-place also contains the ruthless means-orientated types.

7 Personality

Personality is generally taken to refer to the 'more or less stable internal factors that make one person's behaviour consistent from one time to another, and different from the behaviour other people would manifest in comparable situations' (Child, 1968). This definition suggests that personality is a more or less stable attribute of the individual, but not entirely. There is the possibility of continued personality growth and day-to-day short-term fluctuations.

There are a number of problems in dealing with the concept of personality:

1 Is personality an attribute of the individual or something to do with the interaction of the individual with the environment – particularly other people? If personality is interactive, it makes no sense to talk about it without specifying the context. For us, this is not a major stumbling block, since the context is clear – business leaders in their organizations.

2 Is personality a stable characteristic, or does it vary over time? Common-sense observation confirms that for some people personality does vary. Some people act differently at different times or in different situations. Others are always the same, whenever or wherever you meet them. In fact, this variability from 'unpredictable' to 'stable' is one aspect of personality. We have assumed that the personality of our respondents is reasonably stable within the context of work in organizations. Some of the business leaders may also be much the same outside work, others different. This is something we don't know, as it was outside our terms of reference and we did not collect the relevant data.

3 Is personality an innate characteristic or something which is learned? The significance of this is that if personality is innate it cannot be changed. If it is learned, it can be relearned and hence changed. In our view, it is probably a combination of both. However, for this study it probably does not really matter since even if personality is learned the

main learning occurs very early in life, and for most people very little change occurs after they become adults.

In this study, following Child's definition, we consider personality to be a reasonably stable characteristic, within a given setting, in our case 'the business organization'.

MEASURING PERSONALITY

There are two main approaches to defining and measuring personality. First, there are 'type theories' which attempt to classify individuals as one of a range of classes or types. Eysenck and Eysenck (1963), for instance, have suggested a four-part classification based on whether a person is an extrovert or an introvert, and whether he/she is stable or emotional (unstable). This gives four types: stable extrovert, unstable extrovert, stable introvert and unstable introvert. The second approach is via 'trait theory'. Here, the psychologist seeks to define an individual's personality by rating him/her on a series of dimensions, known as traits. In this case, introversion/ extroversion or stable/unstable would simply be one of a possible range of traits. Others could be sociable/unsociable, loyal/fickle or wise/foolish. Many hundreds of adjectives defining traits can be found in the literature, and it is possible to select those which are appropriate for the purpose of the study and, by taking measures on each trait, produce a profile of the individual.

In this study we have used the trait approach, because we believe it gives more flexibility: we can select and measure what we see to be relevant entrepreneurial or intrapreneurial traits. There is also a problem with typologies in that people do not always fit neatly into the categories of the 'type theory'. The trait approach avoids this problem.

Another issue is how to measure the traits in which we are interested. There are basically three possible methods: observation, self-assessment, and psychometric tests and questionnaires. Observing the individuals and trying to assess the degree to which they showed the relevant traits was not possible in this study. Self-assessment, or asking the individuals for their own ratings of themselves, has the problem of subjectivity and can be biased because the individual is unclear about the precise meaning of the trait, although this is a method we have used for some traits, simply because, in this context, there was no alternative. A method we have also used, psychometric tests and questionnaires, is again a form of self-assessment: the individual is asked a series of carefully designed questions, which have been thoroughly tested with a large sample of people. From the responses given, inferences can be drawn concerning the traits shown.

There is a wide popular belief, with some foundation, that responses to interviews and tests of this nature can easily be faked. However, there is also evidence that they produce reasonably accurate pictures of individuals in contexts where there is no reason for faking to occur such as in this study. Our sample were all very successful men and women who would have no need or wish to impress us.

THE PERSONALITY OF THE SUCCESSFUL BUSINESS LEADER

At the end of each interview each respondent was asked if he/she would complete two questionnaires: The Kirton Adaptation/Innovation Inventory and the Kakabadse Political Styles Questionnaire. Not all of them were willing to do so, but 39 did agree. For various reasons some of these failed to complete both questionnaires, so there is some variation in the total number responding in each case.

In addition, the respondents' replies to eight key questions were abstracted from the protocols of the interviews and evaluated by a panel of five independent judges. The statements by interviewees received blind ratings by the judges on bi-polar rating scales appropriate to the specific question. The statements were presented to the judges in a randomized order. The judges' ratings were converted to a standard scores to minimize any individual differences in the use of the rating scales. These scores were then subjected to statistical analysis (i.e. analysis of variance) for each question, with the two groups (entrepreneurs and intrapreneurs) and the judges as factors. The reliability of the judges, using the Generalizability Technique devised by Levy (1974), was 0.9 or higher for all questions. It was thus possible to establish evidence of a 'difference' between entrepreneurs and intrapreneurs, independently of any possible bias on the part of the interviewer. The respondents were asked the following eight questions:

Question 1   Some business leaders say that they are good verbal communicators, others say that they are not so good. How would you describe yourself?

Question 2   Some studies show that entrepreneurs/managers do not work hard at routine work, becoming bored with detail, but work very hard at problem solving. Other studies suggest that this is not the case. What is your opinion?

Question 3   Some business executives talk of having great reserves of psychic/physical energy, others say that they have neither. What have you found?

Question 4   On a continuum of creativity with many good ideas at one end

(100 per cent) and no good ideas at the other where would you place yourself?

Question 5 Some executives have a fear of catastrophic financ others seem immune. What is your experience?

Question 6 Have you ever suffered such a failure?

Question 7 Some business executives attribute part of their success to luck, others don't. What is your experience?

Question 8 On a continuum with risk-seeking at one end (100 per cent) and risk-averse at the other (0 per cent), where would you place yourself?

ADAPTORS OR INNOVATORS

As long ago as 1934, Joseph Schumpeter suggested that the key factor which distinguishes the entrepreneur from the non-entrepreneurial manager is innovation. Schumpeter saw this as a process of 'creative destruction', creating change by acting as a catalyst and interacting with a changing environment. Kirton (1976) takes a more elaborate view noting the existence of two types of manager: (1) those capable of initiating change that improved the current system, but who consistently failed to see possibilities outside the existing system; and (2) 'men of ideas' capable of generating more radical change, but who failed to get their ideas accepted, and so did not succeed in implementing them. He referred to the former as *adaptors* and the latter as *innovators*. In general, 'adaptors' will tend to work within the existing system, while 'innovators' will challenge and change it. There would seem to be quite considerable similarity between Kirton's notion of the innovator and Schumpeter's view of the entrepreneur.

Kirton goes on to say that 'the innovator, in contrast to the adaptor, is liable to be less respectful of the views of others, more abrasive in the presentation of his solution and more at home in a turbulent environment'. 'Adaptors' will more often be found in the more bureaucratic areas of management; 'innovators' tend to be in areas such as research and development.

Where an individual is placed on the continuum from extreme innovator to extreme adaptor depends on the balance of three factors – the degree of *originality* (O), *efficiency* (E) (i.e. the extent to which the person is precise and disciplined) and his/her *rule-group conformity* (R) (i.e. the extent to which the individual is constrained by rules or norms). An adaptor can be quite original (or creative), but will also tend to be high on efficiency (i.e. methodical and precise) and something of a conformist, so that his or her creativity is confined within the system. The innovator, high on originality but low on conformity and efficiency, will be much less constrained by aditional approaches to problems, and so will be more likely to challenge the existing system. The degree to which an individual is an 'adaptor' or an 'innovator' is measured by the Kirton Adaption-Innovation Inventory (KAI). This is organized so that a high score indicates an innovator and a low score an adaptor. In order for this to occur, the subscales are arranged so that a high score indicates high originality, but a *high* E and R score indicate *low* efficiency and conformity respectively.

Owen Oyston on creativity:

Well my difficulty is that it's hellish for the people around me. I'm thinking of ideas all the time, which come out at a fast rate of knots. I get so excited by them. We have just bought a company. I'm the biggest single shareholder with the new merged company and the ideas that have been spilling out of me and my colleagues in the last couple of weeks are legion. We are looking at it in different lights, it's a lateral thinking approach.

Analysis of the KAI results (Table 7.1) shows that the distribution for intrapreneurs is very much the same as for the general population, while entrepreneurs show some bias towards the 'innovator' end of the scale.

Table 7.1 Results of the Kirton Adaptation/Innovation Questionnaire

	Sub-scale scores			Total score
	O	*E*	*R*	
ELITE INDEPENDENT ENTREPRENEURS (N = 19)				
Arithmetic mean	52.2	26.0	26.9	105.2
Standard deviation	5.2	7.5	8.6	
ELITE INTRAPRENEURS (N = 19)				
Arithmetic mean	42.6	21.5	31.3	95.4
Standard deviation	2.3	6.0	9.3	
General UK population	40.8	18.5	35.9	95.0

O = Subscales
E = Efficiency
R = Conformity

Range of possible KAI scores (Kirton, 1976)
32...48...64...80...96...112...128...144...160
Adaptors   Innovators

In the 'originality' subscale, entrepreneurs score as considerably more 'innovative' than intrapreneurs and the general population. This result suggests that entrepreneurs are more likely to challenge the existing system and find novel solutions to problems. A possible reason for this finding could be that independent entrepreneurs may need to be more innovative than the highly successful intrapreneurs, in order to compete successfully in the outside world. Entrepreneurs are, after all, not constrained by an organizational structure of someone else's making and probably enjoy the challenge of creating new or innovative systems. Intrapreneurs, on the other hand, are concerned to maintain an organization which is already running very successfully and may have been doing so for many years. It could be that entrepreneurs who stay too long in an organization that has gone public become more intrapreneurial and less innovative. It appears that once this happens, they become more vulnerable to predators and many are removed. This could account for what happened to some respondents in this study (e.g. Berry, Shah, Bradman and Davies).

On the E (efficiency) scale, intrapreneurs are close to the norm, while entrepreneurs are less efficient. This conforms with the interview data which shows that the entrepreneurs, in general, see themselves as low on attention to detail. Intrapreneurs, concerned with the maintenance of large organizations, possibly have to be more precise and methodical.

The most unexpected score is found on the R scale, with entrepreneurs being more concerned with conformity – though not significantly so – than the general population, while intrapreneurs appear nonconforming. At first sight, it seems strange that people who have set up their own organizations turn out to be more conforming than those who have chosen to work within someone else's. Part of the explanation for this may lie in the origins of many entrepreneurs, who, as we pointed out in Chapter 4, often come from socially marginalized backgrounds. Much of their motivation is to gain acceptance, so they would be very concerned about conforming to rules and norms. Most of our intrapreneurs were born into socially accepted environments and so feel very secure; they can afford to ignore the rules.

A similar, but even more extreme example of this phenomenon was noted by Cox and Cooper (1988) in their study of chief executives. They suggested, however, a different explanation, proposing that the results may be a function of the conditions existing when the data was collected. At the time of their study, British industry had come through a period of major reconstruction. Many of the top intrapreneurs and managers had spent the last four or five years reorganizing their companies, a process involving major change. Many of them had been specifically appointed for this purpose. This same factor may have had some influence on the results of the present study. It is interesting to speculate on whether these less conforming intrapreneurs would still be found at the head of major organizations in a period of stability and steady growth.

TEAM COACH, VISIONARY, TRADITIONALIST OR COMPANY BARON

Kakabadse (1983) has suggested that there are four typical ways in which managers relate to others in the organization, which he refers to as *political styles*. The style a particular manager adopts depends on the mental map which he or she has developed during life. This map depends on two dimensions: perceptions and actions. Kakabadse's perception-action model is shown in Figure 7.1.

The horizontal axis represents the determinants of people's perceptions (i.e. values and beliefs). The two extremes are 'inner-directness' and 'outer-directness'. Individuals who are 'inner directed' develop perceptions and views with little reference to the outside world. Individuals who are 'outer directed' need to comply with perceived attitudes and behaviour that others exhibit in this situation. Complying with the norms of a situation is said to lead to 'shared meaning'. People who need conditions of shared meaning adhere to the values of the organization. Those who generate their own values of life are self-dependent (i.e. they live with unshared meaning). They appreciate that the people with whom they interact may feel differently to themselves, but see little need to adapt to suit others.

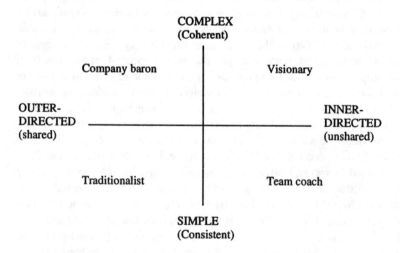

Figure 7.1 The four political styles

Source: Kakabadse (1983)

The vertical axis represents the determinants of people's actions (i.e. their ability to put their views and values into practice). Kakabadse proposes two alternative strategies, simple and complex. Those who adopt a 'simple' strategy aim for consistency. Irrespective of whether the people in the situation work on shared or unshared meaning, the behaviours they feel they should adopt are predictable, commonly recognized and probably previously practised. In this way, individuals are seen to be consistent, and previous experience of those behaviours reduces the degree of felt threat, and does not involve original thought. The key aim for a person practising this strategy is to behave in a manner acceptable to all others in the situation.

Those who adopt a 'complex' strategy behave in ways which they consider suitable to meet their particular needs in the situation. To the outsider, the individual may appear to exhibit no consistent pattern of behaviour. The behaviour may be inconsistent but it is coherent with the individual's desired objectives. Complex action involves new and original ideas and actions, and possibly risk-taking. Based on these dimensions, Kakabadse has defined four stereotyped characters: traditionalist, team coach, company baron and visionary.

Traditionalist

'Traditionalists' wish to fit in with the rest of the organization. They accept the fact that they are dependent on objectives set by others. They accept the way things are done, even if it is detrimental to their own interests. If things have been done in a particular way in the past then that is the way it should continue. 'Traditionalists' will ensure that their group's identity and prevailing attitudes are not threatened with change, for they pay particular attention to the way that new members interact with established members. If someone is seen to behave inappropriately, then some form of reprimand will follow. Despite their group orientation, 'traditionalists' do not like warm friendly relations. Their main concern is with their role. They strive to be 'top dog'.

Team coach

The 'team coach' develops his/her own ideas and beliefs about how to conduct his/her life and affairs. However, independence of thought is not matched by independence of action. The 'team coach' does need to belong to a group of like-minded people and may spend some time searching for the group with whom he/she wishes to associate. A group of smart team coaches could make for an innovative team. They have a capacity for independent thinking and generating new ideas. Team coaches seek a task orientation to their work. Rather than being concerned with personal status, they are concerned with doing their job well.

Company baron

The 'company baron' has two dominant characteristics: (1) an ability to see the total organization as it really is; and (2) a continuous strong drive to enhance his or her position. Both the 'company baron' and the 'visionary' share one strong characteristic – the insight to develop an overview of their organization. This skill enables them to recognize who has power and therefore whom to influence to get what they want. They also know which unspoken norms and values in the organization should never be challenged. Although the 'company baron' has insight into how things are done and why, what he/she finds difficult is to become separate from the majority in the organization. The company baron would be unlikely to introduce changes which would result in a shift of organizational values. One thing is certain: the 'company baron' would never do something unless it suited his/her purpose.

Visionary

The 'visionary' is similar to the company baron in his/her ability to see the organization in total. However, the visionary does not see the same need for loyalty to the company. Not only can the 'visionary' question the way things are done and explore what might be suitable alternatives, but he/she can stand back from the values and views held by the rest of the organization. Visionaries develop their own personal visions and beliefs about the future, and their own philosophies about work and strategies for action. As a result they tend to operate in relative isolation. Sharing personal values is difficult: it is hard to cooperate with someone who has equally well-formed ideas but which stem from separate values. Conflict may arise which may ultimately mean that one of the warring parties will have to leave. They may also feel constrained by the systems in the organization, and this may lead them to be critical of the management or to leave.

Kakabadse (1983) presents a questionnaire which can be used to assess the political style of any individual. Nineteen entrepreneurs and 20 intrapreneurs completed this. The results are shown in Table 7.2. As can be seen, the entrepreneurs were predominantly 'team coaches' and 'visionaries', while the intrapreneurs tended to be 'traditionalists' or 'company barons'. The implication is that entrepreneurs are 'inner directed' and operate on unshared meanings, while intrapreneurs are more 'outer directed' and work with shared meanings. This would clearly seem to relate to the fact that the latter work their way up within an existing organization and the former set up their own. Both groups divide equally in terms of their use of simple or complex action strategies.

There do seem to be differences between intrapreneurial managers and independent entrepreneurs in terms of political repertoire. Four of the intrapreneurs identified 'team coach' as their most dominant style, and three described themselves as 'visionary'. In contrast, ten of the independent entrepreneurs identified themselves as having the dominant characteristics of the 'visionary' political style, while eleven were shown to have a 'team coach' style, with only one being identified as a 'company baron'. No entrepreneurs were identified as being 'traditionalists'. In summary the results suggest the following styles:

Entrepreneurs	Intrapreneurs
More of a 'team coach'	More 'traditional'
More 'visionary'	More of a 'company baron'

White, Cox and Cooper (1992) found that their sample of successful women were either 'team coaches' or 'visionaries'. There were no 'traditionalists' or 'company barons'. They point out that both 'visionaries' and 'team coaches' are inner directed and develop their perceptions and views with little reference to the outside world. Inner-directed individuals generate

Table 7.2 Political styles of entrepreneurs and intrapreneurs

	Traditionalist	Team coach	Company baron	Visionary
First choice of styles				
Entrepreneurs	0	11	1	10
Intrapreneurs	5	4	9	3
ENTREPRENEURS				
Means	12.15	21.89	13.68	21.63
Standard deviation	3.98	4.34	4.10	3.77
INTRAPRENEURS				
Means	17.95	15.05	21.57	15.38
Standard deviation	6.45	8.41	6.31	6.00

(Entrepreneurs N = 19); (Intrapreneurs N = 20)

Some respondents had two first equal styles, hence the totals are greater than the number of respondents.

their own values in life. Much the same could be said about the entrepreneurs in the current study. Perhaps the characteristic which the two groups (women managers and women entrepreneurs in general) have in common is that they both see themselves battling against a somewhat hostile world made up of individuals who are rather different from themselves, and who have very different values.

The intrapreneurs, on the other hand, who tend to be 'traditionalists' or 'company barons', are 'outer directed', taking their values and perceptions from those around them. They are much more conformist, prepared to accept the objectives of others, and concerned to 'fit in' with the organization, although, in the case of 'company barons', many also have a desire to dominate. These are all characteristics which make the intrapreneur more suited to managing a large well-established organization than striking out and starting a new one.

VERBAL COMMUNICATORS

We were interested in finding out how the respondents rated their ability as verbal communicators, and what difference, if any, existed between entrepreneurs and intrapreneurs. As noted above, all the respondents were asked the following question: 'Some business leaders say that they are good verbal communicators, others say that they are not so good. How would you describe yourself?'

In the statistical analysis carried out on the respondents' answers to this question, we found no significant difference between entrepreneurs and intrapreneurs. This result is consistent with previous research, and is not a surprising finding. Independent entrepreneurs starting from lowly beginnings need to convince others of their ability and of their ideas if they want to attract venture capital. To do this they must be good verbal communicators. Intrapreneurs, on the other hand, who have taken over the family business, have usually been subjected to a 'vetting' procedure, either by the family or by board members, or both. Intrapreneurs in family or non-family businesses also need to be good communicators in order to motivate their workforce and communicate their plans.

BORED WITH ROUTINE WORK

Several studies (McClelland, 1967; Kets de Vries, 1977; Silver, 1986) have indicated that entrepreneurs become bored with routine work. We wanted to find out who in our sample of business leaders became bored with detail or routine work, and if there was a significant difference in attitude between the two groups. The question put to the respondents was as follows: 'Some studies show that entrepreneurs/managers do not work hard at routine work, becoming bored with detail, but work very hard at problem solving. Other studies suggest that this is not the case. What is your opinion?'

Analysis of the answers showed that there was a highly significant difference between the two groups. Entrepreneurs become significantly more bored with doing routine work than intrapreneurs. This is consistent with McClelland's (1967) finding that while entrepreneurs became bored with routine work they worked harder at problem solving, and with Silver's (1986) suggestion that entrepreneurs 'just never have sufficient time to enter into such activities'.

It seems strange that people who have built a large-scale organization from the ground up should be significantly less concerned with the detail than those who have chosen to work within someone else's organization or those who act as stewards of a family business. After all, the independent entrepreneur's firm can be seen as an extension of the entrepreneur's personality, and many studies, including Levinson's (1971), report that the founders of these enterprises find it extremely difficult to 'let go'. But the requirements of a business change with its size and the stages of its development. Initially, the entrepreneur must be concerned with all aspects of his/her enterprise. However, large and expanding, organizations require a more structured management system than small ones. The owner who does everything him/herself cannot possibly develop the company into a major corporation. In order to develop organizations as large as those in this study, the leader must delegate and leave details to others, while he/she develops new aspects of the business. The entrepreneur who does not do this remains simply the proprietor of a small business.

This difference between the entrepreneurial and intrapreneurial approach is well illustrated by David Jones, when describing how he and George Davies worked together. They were, at the time, joint managing directors of NEXT. Asked if he became bored with routine work, Jones replied:

> No, I'm more of a routine person. Again, just to show you a comparison, we have recently launched the NEXT Directory. We had a small group of people, directors, who were involved with different aspects of it. George [Davies] would sit down and have a meeting to discuss where we were going. The Directory is now on the straight and narrow and everything is sorted out. Now George had said to me, Will you look after all those meetings? Because he [George] has gone on to something else, so you see we are a team. He is the front runner and he comes up with a lot of the new creative ideas, whereas I'm quite happy to handle the detail and make sure it works. So to answer your question, I don't mind detailed routine work.

RESERVES OF PHYSICAL AND/OR PSYCHIC ENERGY

We introduced the following question after a pilot study had shown that many entrepreneurs talk about having great reserves of energy: 'Some business executives talk of having great reserves of psychic/physical energy, others say that they have neither. What have you found?'

The answers show a highly significant difference between the groups, with the entrepreneurs reporting greater reserves of psychic/physical energy. Typical entrepreneur's answers showed great enthusiasm:

> We all [entrepreneurs] have great reserves of energy. If you enjoy what you are doing the energy is created within you.
>
> (Sir David Alliance)

> I think that to be a successful businessman you have to have a great deal of energy because unless you are energized you are not going to get anywhere.
>
> (Gerald Ronson)

> Looking back, I would say that I had energy . . . I found life exciting.
>
> (Michael Guthrie)

> I work 16 hours a day, I think that explains it.
>
> (George Davies)

> Yes, yes, I sometimes feel as though I'm going to burst.
>
> (Emma Nicholson)

Many intrapreneurs made no claims to energy. For example, David Jones said: 'No, I don't, to be honest. I probably release my energies in a quieter way.' Many often simply said 'no, neither' in response to this question.

The energy levels of entrepreneurs can be summed up by Owen Oyston:

> It's not just energy, energy is important because without it you can't do it, you need the energy, but energy drives us into other areas. I think that it's a combination . . . it's a restless soul approach . . . where you are never satisfied, you are always looking to new horizons, you need another shot of adrenalin – that involves an acquisition, it involves growth, it involves high exposure, it involves a high profile. And so you go on and on. The majority of people would be more than satisfied with certain achievements. I think the most single common element between people like Eddie Shah and myself is that we are probably egotists, we want to prove to the world that we are 'special people'. I say that, even though, in many ways I recognize the many weaknesses I have.
>
> The biggest single thing really is this driving force and the fact that you cannot relax. I can never relax; seven days a week I have to work,

it's the Protestant ethic which militates against me, and it's the environment, where I learned that work was an essential ingredient in life and you satisfied both yourself and other people if you committed yourself to it. I suppose that it is a disease almost, but I cannot find, nor wish to have, time off to go away and relax and have a holiday. I have to be working and the work-load gets greater. It's never got easier and it's a question of very hard work and long hours, that's how I've achieved it. There is no magic formula, no clever mechanism.

MOTIVATION

Since the entrepreneur made claims to having considerable energy, we explored further the sources of this energy and the possible differences in motivation between intrapreneur and entrepreneur. All the interviewees were asked to rank the following four motivations with respect to their real-world goals: power, wealth, the need to achieve, and independence. Table 7.3 shows the first choice of motivation for each group. The response to each possible motive is discussed in more detail below.

Power

Not one entrepreneur ranked 'power' as a cardinal goal worth seeking, whereas 9 per cent of intrapreneurs saw this as one of their main goals. However, generally, both groups said that they saw 'power' as lying in the hands of others – their employees – and that it was given to the leader in order to carry out tasks. This 'power', the interviewees intimated, could just as easily be taken away. The ranking suggests that intrapreneurs are more likely to rank 'power' as a principal motivation than are entrepreneurs. It seems difficult to accept the interviewees' argument that power is fragile, transient or fleeting, and depends upon the ability of the wielder of that power to use it correctly, when we have seen the 'power' of such

Table 7.3 First choice of motivation for entrepreneurs and intrapreneurs

	Entrepreneurs	*Intrapreneurs*
Power	0	2
Wealth	4	7
Need to achieve	9	10
Independence	6	3
Totals	19	22

Victor Kiam II on dreams:

I still have many dreams that I would like to fulfil. I think we live in a world of fantasy. Just recently I was able to purchase the New England Patriots football team, which is a member of the National Football League. I never really believed that I would be in a position to acquire such a team, and obviously this is a fulfilment of a fantasy, not a worthwhile financial investment.

N.B. Victor Kiam II has recently sold the Patriots.

people as Robert Maxwell and his unrestricted ability to use and abuse it as he alone saw fit. There was never any question or removal of power from him, until he decided to relinquish it.

Wealth

Twenty-one per cent of entrepreneurs saw 'wealth' as a primary goal, but this was usually qualified by explanations of why they needed wealth. Wealth was seen as liberating, giving the entrepreneur the independence needed to achieve some greater goal. Intrapreneurs, on the other hand, saw wealth as a reward for their effort and as providing security in an uncertain world. These views would seem to relate to their lower levels of risk taking, discussed below. Out of the four choices, intrapreneurs rank wealth higher as a goal than entrepreneurs.

Need to achieve

Forty-seven per cent of entrepreneurs felt a strong desire to achieve: 'to show that other lot' (Davies) or 'to prove to the world that I could do it' (de Savary). This 'need to achieve' for entrepreneurs has an echo of strong parental influences on the child. Intrapreneurs also ranked the 'need to achieve' top (46 per cent), but for different reasons. Intrapreneurs as chairmen/women of leading, or notable, family firms wanted to see their stewardship of the firm as more productive than the last chairperson's: 'I want some little spot in history so they will say, well he wasn't Prime Minister but at least he wasn't a bad chairman' (Pilkington).

Oyston on motivation:

Well the wealth is not a factor so I would cross it out straight away. It really is not a factor, it never has been. It gives you freedom to do what you want but that comes as a result of commercial success. If you are talking in terms of what you are aiming for, I never aim for wealth. But when I've got it I use it as a tool, as a bricklayer would use a trowel and bricks, or as a joiner would use a plane. The need to achieve is the paramount thing. Power, yes; bluntly, power is part of my adrenalin, it's part of the make-up, it's part of what makes it all worthwhile. If you have control of an organization with thousands of people, then clearly, people perceive you as someone who has status, as someone who can help, as someone who contributes to society. I mean, that's what led me into radio, the fact that I wanted to be perceived, not as making money, but perceived by the community as someone who wanted to put something back into it. Independence, if I thought about it, you are probably right. I think that wealth does give you independence . . . I don't think that you could operate in a framework where you are under control. I mean, I do have all kinds of controls and restraints in my life and I am mindful of it daily, for example the Cable Authority, the IBA, the local authorities. I mean, everything that you do, there are areas of control, the press watch every move you make. It does make you a very cautious person and you are aware that if you step out of line you could get a bloody nose. That's the price you pay, of course.

Independence

Entrepreneurs ranked independence second highest, at 32 per cent. For entrepreneurs, independence is that factor which allows them to achieve their goals and reach for their dreams. Independence allowed Jeffrey Archer to 'write' while fuelling his 'dream to be Prime Minister'. Intrapreneurs rank independence relatively low (14 per cent). Because of the high proportion of family firms in the sample, their general focus was stability over time for their company. Stability in this sense can perhaps be seen as being restrictive, and so reducing the level of independence.

CREATIVITY

Both groups were also asked: 'On a continuum of creativity with many good ideas at one end (100 per cent) and no good ideas at the other (0 per cent), where would you place yourself?' Entrepreneurs saw themselves as significantly more creative than intrapreneurs. These findings are totally consistent with the results from the Kirton Adaptation/Innovation Inventory, discussed earlier in this chapter. Some typical examples of the respondents' answers are given below. Those from the entrepreneurs illustrate their very high self-rating on creativity, linking with their higher scores on innovation:

> I would place myself 80 to 85 per cent on the scale towards creativity. It starts with imagination. It is brought down to earth with practicality.
>
> (Victor Kiam II)

> Oh I'm an ideas person. I have a reputation for having ten ideas before breakfast.
>
> (Lord Young)

> All actors are creative, I feel. As an actor and a businessman I think I'm creative.
>
> (Owen Oyston)

> Yes, I created a new method of producing newspapers.
>
> (Eddy Shah)

> It depends what you mean by good ideas. I keep thinking of ideas and then they disappear. But I suppose in terms of truly creative ideas, every decision that has been made in this organization has come from an idea that has been originally created by me.
>
> (Tony Berry)

The intrapreneurs, on the other hand, see themselves as much more managers of other people's creativity:

> I'm not creative; my job as manager was to support creative people.
>
> (The late Lord McAlpine of Moffat)

> Sixty to 65 per cent. I'm best putting ideas together into coherent policies . . . my forecasts have been accurate but I'm not sure about real creativity.
>
> (Sir Adrian Cadbury)

FEAR OF FAILURE

It was considered important to ask about failure and fear of failure in order to understand how business leaders lived with, recovered from and coped with business failure. Two questions were asked of all our respondents:

'Some executives have a fear of catastrophic financial failure, others seem immune. What is your experience?' This was followed by: 'Have you ever suffered such a failure?'

Analysis of the answers to the question on fear of failure indicated that the entrepreneurs had a significantly greater fear than did the intrapreneurs. Kets de Vries (1977) also found that many entrepreneurs had this fear, and with hindsight entrepreneurs of relatively newly established businesses in the 1980s had good reason to fear. Many such businesses have subsequently failed. Analysis of the answers to the question on actual failure revealed that the entrepreneurs were, again, significantly more likely to have experienced financial failure.

Catastrophic financial failure and fear of failure were, then, suffered mainly by the entrepreneur. Why is this so? Some of the answers given by each group may provide some insight. Peter Gummer, founder of the largest PR firm in the world, for example, discloses that: 'One of the main things entrepreneurs don't talk about is their continual fear and insecurity.' Another entrepreneur, Owen Oyston, says: 'I fear financial failure. It's something I could not cope with. That's what drives me on.'

We are reminded here of what Kets de Vries (1977) has suggested about some entrepreneurs and their 'death wish': 'the entrepreneur emerges as an anxious individual, a non-conformist, poorly organized and not a stranger to self-destructive behaviour'. Their business operations seem to be characterized by patterns of elation and despair, of success and failures: this may be an example of what Schumpeter (1931) has called the *creative destructor*. It appears that failure is, in part, expected, and success perceived as a prelude to failure.

Sir Mark Weinberg set up a division in Hambro Life to examine acquisitions in the light of their potential contribution to catastrophic financial failure. In the end, this fear of failure led him to sell out to the British American Tobacco Company.

The degree of concern with failure is viewed differently by some entrepreneurs. Victor Kiam, when answering questions on risk and failure replied that he saw himself as a high risk taker. However, when Kiam addressed the fear of failure, he goes on to say that:

I think if an individual, whether he is an entrepreneur or not, doesn't fear catastrophic financial failure, then there must be something wrong with the individual. I do believe you place yourself in a position to minimize the potential for catastrophic financial failure.

There are exceptions. Eddy Shah, for instance, says of financial failure: 'It has never worried me. I never contemplate failure. Half of me is Eastern, so here is a bit of the "Inshalla" (God willing) peace in me.' Shah, as a leading entrepreneur who has come back from two financial failures, was asked to elaborate on why some people fear business failure more than others:

> I will tell you what I told *The Times* a few weeks ago. I said that in America a manager that had failed was looked upon by the investors as someone who had learned a damn good lesson and they are prepared to risk on him next time. He has learned by his mistakes. But here, as soon as somebody fails, they put a big stamp of failure on him, and suddenly he is the pariah of society. What they don't realize is that the guy has learned more by failing – nobody is going to be successful all the time. This is, basically, because many Americans have come up the hard way. They have not got the tremendous inherited wealth we have over here. Also, there is not the class system over in the USA – OK, you've got the 400 families or so around Massachusetts, but apart from that, basically in America, people operate in their own time, or their father's time, or their grandfather's time scale, but not beyond that. In this time slot, they have seen families make and lose wealth. America is a much more fluid society, there is no class culture as such; there's a money barrier but not a class barrier, as we have here. So, the incentives are there if you want to do well.

Robert Gavron, the entrepreneur who founded St Ives printing with £5,000 in 1964 and is currently the largest shareholder in the company, with over £25 million worth of shares, recalls that he has overcome his fear of failure by pragmatic, long-range planning.

> I must say that I don't have a fear of that [catastrophic failure]. But then I did have a fear of that when I was much younger, so, therefore, I've spread my risk. You see I'm risk-averse. Of course, if the whole world collapses, then I'll collapse. If only part of the world collapses, I'll be one of the last to go. I have overcome that fear by providing for it.

Perhaps this, and other entrepreneurs' ability to bounce back from failure – a clearly demonstrated characteristic – is explained by David Silver (1986):

> Courage is visible. People can sense leadership and courage in others and they flock to those persons. Courage is the counterbalance for fear. The successful entrepreneur is not blind to possible failure. On the contrary, he knows well about the forces that lead to the collapse of the company he is building.

What the entrepreneur has learned from failure is never to be mesmerised by the lingering chance of failure.

In contrast to entrepreneurs, intrapreneurs see failure from a different perspective. The stability over time of Pilkington Glass has allowed its current chairman, Sir Antony Pilkington, to reflect: 'We are a very well found company. We have both strength and depth and we will never face catastrophic failure.'

We can say that, in general, entrepreneurs in this study show very similar qualities to those described by Gilder (1986):

> From their knowledge of failure they forge success. In accepting risk they achieve security for all. In embracing change they ensure social and economic stability. While the entitled children see failure as catastrophe – a reason to resign – the entrepreneur takes it in his stride as a spur to new struggle.

The independent entrepreneurs' ability to overcome failure and setbacks is truly awesome, as demonstrated throughout this study. They do not seem to understand *how* to lose. Perhaps their attitude is best summed up by the response of one interviewee, Daniel Rose, when asked about his attitude to failure:

> Would a salmon going upstream to spawn consider that its failure to leap one rapid, one time is a failure?

LUCK

Both groups were asked if luck had played an important part in their success. The responses showed that entrepreneurs were less likely to attribute their achievements to luck than were intrapreneurs, who were more likely to do so, for at least part of their success. Only 26 per cent of entrepreneurs attributed a significant part of their success to luck, compared with 63 per cent of the intrapreneurs. These results are consistent with the entrepreneurs having a higher 'internal' locus of control (Rotter, 1966) or, as Whyte (1956) describes it, an 'internal gyroscope'.

Jeffrey Archer, for example, sees luck as playing very little part in his entrepreneurial activities: 'Five per cent is luck and 95 per cent you do yourself.' Harold Woolf, like Archer, is not convinced that luck and entrepreneurship have anything in common:

> No, luck is bullshit, but sometimes you look for things to turn your way. I have had various instances in my life where maybe I've got planning consent for something and people would look at me and say, 'that lucky so-and-so'. But I know that when I went into it, I thought to myself: if the downside is very little and the upside is fairly good, and I get planning consent, it will be great.

Sir David Alliance argues along similar lines when he says 'You create your own luck in business', or as Eddy Shah put it 'the world is a rat race and the smartest rat wins'.

Teresa Gorman, however, takes a more complex view:

> Luck, I feel, is a combination of preparation and talent, so I do not know if there is such a thing as luck by itself. OK, you can talk about serendipity and that certainly helps you get off the ground. In my case I got a whacking great order out of the Open University, and that helped me enormously. Otherwise, I might have run out of funds, and steam, and had to pack up, but that got me going. All through my life I've been 'lucky' like that.

Francis Bailey takes a slightly less extreme position, feeling that luck is necessary, but that there is more to success than luck alone: 'This area has grown tremendously and may be I happened to be in the right place at the right time, but you can't depend on luck alone, you have to do something.'

The different assumptions about luck made by the intrapreneurs can be illustrated by the following quotations. For instance, one respondent said: 'I see myself in my present field by a stroke of dumb luck – a stroke of good fortune.' Or Martin Laing: 'Yes, being born into the family was luck. I suppose I had no control over that. There is no doubt about it, being in the right spot at the right time is everything.'

However, not all intrapreneurs considered that luck had played any part in their success. Emma Nicholson, for instance, recalls that, 'Luck had nothing to do with my business. I don't know what luck is and it has not touched me anyway.'

Victor Kiam II on luck:

The acquisition of Remington took place because I was reading *Business Week* on a Saturday and noticed that the former chairman of Sperry had stated in an article that he would rather sell one Univac than 100,000 shavers. I followed that up on Monday morning and was able to acquire the company. Was it luck that I read the article? Was it entrepreneurship that I was able to seize upon the idea and follow it through? Or was it just plain hard work?

There is a very important aspect to being an entrepreneur, and that is timing. Sometimes the situation is not right for whatever you are planning to undertake, but subsequently it can be. I might add that the only things that I have regretted are the things that I have not done.

It may be that the apparently differing views expressed here are simply different sides of the same coin. Many of both groups did acknowledge the importance of luck as well as the need for effort. Perhaps, as Goethe said, 'He who seizes the right moment is the right man.' That is, that good luck is an opportunity for which the 'right man' must be prepared, or alternatively, if one is prepared, then good luck is an opening to be exploited. What our sample are undoubtedly good at is seizing opportunities.

Ellen Langer (1980) argues that some people are considerably more inventive than others; individuals differ in their ability to cross boundaries and in the frequency with which they can break the norms of behaviour. These individuals fail to make the distinction between skill and chance elements, because of their simultaneous presence. If we allow that every skill situation contains some elements of chance, and that every chance situation contains some skill elements, we can argue that the more someone tries to do something and understands the relationships in what he or she is doing, the 'better' or 'luckier' they may become, depending on your viewpoint. This is illustrated by Shah when recalling a game of golf he played with Gary Player:

Peter Gummer on fortuitous happenings:

Let me give you my favourite quotation of all time. Armand Hammer, 87 years of age, was being interviewed on television. The interviewer said to him: 'Doctor, you have made fortune after fortune in the past, and several multi-billion-dollar fortunes in your life. What role has luck played in this?'

He looked at the interviewer and said, 'When you work 24 hours a day, seven days a week, you tend to be lucky.'

My wife pulls my leg saying, 'You scramble out of bed at 5.30 a.m. every morning, in spite of the terrible times that you have had. You still get to the office at seven o'clock. You still have all these meetings, and do day trips to America, and travel to the Far East, but despite all the problems you have, you do it all with a smile upon your face – but of course, you do tend to be lucky.'

[In reality] it's because I'm there! I'm out there, I'm mixing it. I'm trying hard all the time! You're looking at everything, you never switch off. There is that lovely old saying: you have to kiss a hell of a lot of frogs before you find a prince. I never listen to those people who tell me that you can get away with working three or four hours a day. If you are not doing a 15 or 16 or 17-hour day, you can't be out there, doing the things that have to be done. You simply can't be there!

Gary Player, probably the greatest bunker player in the world, did one of his usual chip-ins, and this woman said to him 'Mr Player, that's amazing, you were so lucky to chip-in.' And he said, 'I know and isn't it funny, the more I practise the luckier I become'.

RISK

All respondents were asked the following question relating to financial/monetary risk: 'On a continuum with risk-seeking at one end (100 per cent) and risk-averse at the other (0 per cent), where would you place yourself?'

Analysis of the answers shows that entrepreneurs rated themselves as significantly more risk-seeking than intrapreneurs. Seventy-four per cent of elite independent entrepreneurs placed themselves around the 75 per cent mark, whereas only 32 per cent of elite intrapreneurs located themselves above the 50 per cent mark, with these considering themselves as 'calculated or average risk-takers'. Associated with the characteristic of self-sufficiency is the acceptance of challenges involving risk. The entrepreneurs see risk-taking as a fundamental aspect of entrepreneurship, and our interviews highlight this point.

Intrapreneurs in their early challenging assignments were often risky, but it is important that this was not seen generally as a gamble: it was always a calculated risk seen to be within the acceptable limits of the individual's skills and abilities.

The independent entrepreneurs seemed to almost enjoy risk for its own sake, as something that stimulates the flow of adrenalin and makes them feel alive again. For example, Jennifer d'Abo, argues:

If you want people to really grow, then they have to take some risks and you have to support them when they get into trouble. The ones who race

---

Peter de Savary on risk:

I suppose I'm a risk-seeker. Business is like chess and you'll find a lot of entrepreneurs play chess; if they don't play chess, they play backgammon. It's something that you are born with, it's not something you can ever learn. It's really the thrill of the chase and the sport of the game, and therefore the risk is the odds you put yourself against. You have to measure the risk and look at the risk–reward ratios and determine whether for that reward, for that risk, you can win. It's that thrill that motivates you.

along the flat will never go over the hill. They will be the big company men. They will need someone else, with a plan, to lift them to the next level. Richard Branson is a man I really admire because he is a great, great marketing man. He wasn't trained as a marketing man, he just does it right. He is giving us what we want on airlines.

Archer explains his notion of risk as follows:

> Entrepreneurs are all risk-takers, they are the Walter Raleighs, the Francis Drakes. They are all pirates really, but Britain's strength was at being pirates . . . the modern pirates are Jimmy Goldsmith, James Hanson, etc. . . . they command ships, win battles and beat the enemy.

Teresa Gorman argues that: 'In business you have to take a risk because you believe in what your product or service is. In essence you back yourself.' Both Davies and Shah would agree with Gorman. According to Davies: 'If the right deal came along I would still risk it all.' And Eddy Shah says that: 'When you start in business you take way-out risks.'

Owen Oyston, moving towards a more calculated risk position, states: 'I think that in most businesses that I have acquired, you have to remove the risk . . . but sometimes you have to make a decision based on guts.' Peter de Savary comments: 'I take risks and enter into commitments that could potentially destroy me. The vast majority of people never do such things.'

One exception in this group is Sir Nigel Broackes, who places himself at the 51 per cent mark. The responses of intrapreneurs are in the main typical of that made by Rose, Pilkington, Schroder and Burrough. They see risk differently: 'Risk, I feel,' says Daniel Rose, 'is closely linked to the attribute of curiosity, which itself becomes, in a rationalized form, the urge

---

Victor Kiam II on risk:

I've always opted for high risk reward ratios. I still do. I don't think, if anything, I've lessened the risk-taking. As a matter of fact, years ago I had to look to the support of a wife and three children, and to make sure, as best I could, that their future was not placed in jeopardy. It was perhaps a deterrent in the entrepreneurial effort. Today I no longer have those constraints and, having reached a level of financial security, I can embark on programmes or endeavours which I would probably not have done years ago.

to discover and to innovate . . . which by any standard is a positive virtue.'
Sir Antony Pilkington described risk as follows:

> I think that risk is a function of size. It is easier to be an entrepreneur if
> you are a one-man-band. The bigger the operation that you are
> managing, the fewer risks you are likely to take.

Another intrapreneur explains '[I'm] risk averse, but it depends upon the
underlying motivation.' And Emma Nicholson says:

> Risk: I would place myself in the middle. I believe that methodical
> risk-taking is crucial to successful initiative; if you are not taking risks
> you are not trying hard enough. On the other hand, a continuing business
> has to grow on a steady basis and the largest proportions of decisions
> have to be without risk. There is a great deal of fun in taking risks, but
> you are not there for yourself but to advance the business.

Another exception in this group would be Sam Whitbread, who is an
above-average risk-taker, placing himself at the 70 per cent mark.

Of course, even independent entrepreneurs research the situation and
calculate the downside, but they do see themselves as high risk takers and
give the impression that it is an aspect of their lives which has considerable
appeal. This is certainly not always the case. During the interview with
Lord Hanson's assistant, John Pattisson, it was suggested that Lord Hanson
made every effort to eliminate risk from the business equation and that he
was fundamentally risk averse. Correspondence with Professor R. Lynn
(20 November 1986), author of *The Entrepreneurs* concurs with these
findings: 'It is a cliché that entrepreneurs are risk-takers and in my opinion
this is a misconception. It is important to distinguish between limited and
unlimited risks.'

However, Frank Knight (1940) views the entrepreneur as a taker of
decisions involving non-quantifiable uncertainties. Kets de Vries (1977)
argues that, with the split of ownership and management, in the use of other
than the entrepreneur's personal capital sources, such as those of venture
capitalists, the entrepreneur can be considered more a *creator* of risk than
the *taker* of it, as he/she enters marginal markets or develops innovative
products.

Although the entrepreneur does not necessarily bear the financial risk of
an enterprise, he is exposed to a considerable degree of social and psychological risks. The purgatory of entrepreneurship can be a time of extreme
hardship during which considerable psychological sacrifices are endured.
Naturally, a certain tolerance for economic risk is necessary, but a tolerance for psychological risks might be more important.

It was noticeable, however, that even some independent entrepreneurs move away from risky challenges toward calculated risk-taking, as they became better established, more socially aware and had more to lose. Ronson, Berry, Sir David Alliance and Peter de Savary, all well established multi-millionaires, say that they have become less risky over the years because they realize that many hundreds of thousands of their employees depend upon their entrepreneurial actions for their livelihood. Berry puts this point most succinctly when he stated: 'I'm a risk-taker, but remember that the higher you climb . . . the less risks you are going to take. There is just no point in taking great risks once you are successful.'

EXECUTIVE SUMMARY

This chapter has examined a number of personality characteristics on which entrepreneurs differ from intrapreneurs. The key differences are as follows:

- On the Kirton Adaptation/Innovation Inventory, entrepreneurs show very high levels of innovation. Intrapreneurs score very close to the population norm, being neither strongly innovators or adaptors.
- Intrapreneurs are close to average on efficiency (being methodical and precise).
- Entrepreneurs are much less efficient.
- Entrepreneurs are much more conformist than intrapreneurs.
- In terms of Kakabadse's political styles, entrepreneurs are mainly 'team coaches' or 'visionaries'. Intrapreneurs are more often found to be 'traditionalists' or 'company barons'.
- Both groups see themselves as good verbal communicators.
- Entrepreneurs easily become bored with routine work; intrapreneurs are more able to deal with detail.
- Entrepreneurs see themselves as having great reserves of energy. Intrapreneurs seem to have this characteristic to a lesser extent.
- Both groups see themselves as motivated by a need to achieve, but entrepreneurs have a higher need of independence, and intrapreneurs higher needs of wealth and power.
- Entrepreneurs see themselves as more creative than do the intrapreneurs.
- Entrepreneurs have a greater fear of failure and are much more likely to have experienced catastrophic financial failure than are intrapreneurs.
- Entrepreneurs do not attribute their success to luck. Intrapreneurs are much more likely to do so.
- Entrepreneurs see themselves as much higher risk-takers than do intrapreneurs.

The general picture which emerges is of two groups who are both highly skilled high achievers. The entrepreneur appears as a somewhat mercurial individual, something of an outsider, internally motivated, very active and challenging, a high risk-taker, but concerned about failure. The intra-preneur is a more predictable person, more careful and controlled, more confident, more externally motivated – very much an 'organization man'.

norms of behaviour derived from parents and from religious teachings of moral obligation.

Peter Gummer on philanthropy:

There are two separate aspects to philanthropy. First there is the provision of money, and second is the provision of time. My wife and I have a large family and our first priority lies there, with the children.

[That aside] we actually tie-up a percentage of our income . . . Saying, we will give 'X' per cent of our income every year, in any way we choose, to a whole realm of different things that we think are interesting.

We review our 'giving' every year, and we try not to 'give' in between. If somebody writes me a letter and says: 'Would you give me £1,000 to help the cancer research organization?' we write back and say: 'No. We will think about your letter, and we will look at it again in six, nine or ten months' time.'

The second thing we do, however, is convenant our time. So we say to ourselves, we will always give 'X' number of hours to do things. This second area is the area where we gain most. I have spoken to a charity this morning. I'm sure that the half-hour advice which I gave to help sort out a problem is worth far more than £1–2,000. So you see, I'm a great believer in the time commitment, of using the business and professional skills which I have acquired, and using those attributes for the benefit of other individuals. Although what I'm about to say exaggerates the point – I still believe that it's easy to give money, but it's far more difficult to give time.

[You give] because you have a skill, you have acquired judgement and . . . you should contribute to society's decision-making process. Because you have acquired those skills, you can benefit a larger group of people by helping them to manage their resources wisely, than you can by giving them a hell of a lot of money. I suppose, it boils down to fulfilling your obligation . . . to good neighbourliness, if you like.

There is, by the way, a P.S. to that. It goes back to the question on luck. The thing that I have found about charitable or public service work is the wide range of other contacts you develop. Don't let anybody tell you that this is some great, totally altruistic kind of thing; it's immensely helpful to the 'giver' also, because you meet a wide range of people that you would never, ever, ordinarily meet under any other circumstances. And you can find them jolly interesting, helpful and useful.

8   Philanthropy

Acts of philanthropy have always been associated with entrepreneurs. This was never more true than in the Victorian era. There are many examples of extreme levels of entrepreneurial good works from this period. One good example would be the work of Sir Titus Salt (1803–76), in many ways the archetypal Victorian industrialist/entrepreneur. Bradley (1987) sees him rising from comparatively humble beginnings and, by dint of hard work and business acumen, becoming one of the richest and most powerful of the West Riding textile barons, employing over 3,500 workers. As an employer, Salt an active Congregationalist, was also a paternalist, taking his workers out of the polluted environment of Bradford and providing them with good housing and amenities, but expecting them in return to be sober, God-fearing and hard working. Salt spent the latter 23 years of his life building Saltaire – a model industrial community in the countryside. Bradley suggests that Salt's motives were a mixture of sound business sense and philanthropy.

None of our interviewees matched the philanthropic acts of the Victorians. None of our respondents have constructed a Port Sunlight village, like William Hesketh Lever, and we found no Titus Salt in our sample. There were no Jesse Boots to provide parks on the banks of the Trent or buildings and facilities for the University College of Nottingham. There were no George Cadburys to build model villages like Bournville for their workers, and provide an environment so that 'no man ought to be compelled to live where a rose cannot grow' (Bradley, 1987).

Although we did not find a Lever or a Salt or a Cadbury – perhaps because they are no longer necessary in Britain – we did find many acts of philanthropy, generosity and charity. Such acts were, we found, entered into almost equally by both the entrepreneurs and 'intrapreneurs, with 50 per cent of all respondents declaring acts of pro-social behaviour. The interviews suggest that these acts stem mainly from their own internalized

I wouldn't want you to go away with the idea that there is some high moral tone in what I'm saying, because I don't think that there is one. I think that there is an ulterior motive – if that's the right word – which means that you continue to network. You continue to build contacts, and people say: 'Well, he has been jolly helpful over this, maybe we can help him out with that.'

The people you meet tend to be multi-faceted people with lots of other interests and that's the advantage of it. I actually find it an extremely valuable exercise. Lots of people who I would never have met have helped to sell our business because they don't like going elsewhere.

However, not all our respondents saw themselves as philanthropists. When asked about why acts of philanthropy were undertaken by some entrepreneurs, Eddy Shah, for example, replied:

I don't think there's a set answer. I suppose some people do it because they want to be loved. Others because they feel they should give a little back to society, others, no doubt, to get knighthoods and peerages . . . lots of people do it for tax reasons.

Owen Oyston sees 'giving' as being directly related to guilt: 'It's guilt, it's all a question of guilt.' Oyston, however, is responsible for both public and private acts of 'giving'. He was anonymously responsible for the release of many of the Liverpool soccer fans held in a Belgium prison because they couldn't raise the bail money for their release after the Hysal Stadium disaster.

Less private was Oyston's attempt to save the socialist newspaper, *News on Sunday*.

I was invited to look at the *News on Sunday* which was losing, at the

---

Peter de Savary on philanthropy:

One is so materially successful, also one sees so much suffering and deprivation in the world there is a sort of guilt feeling, sub-consciously. I think that part of it is in one's nature. You imagine that you have taken a lot out and you just feel that, in a calculated way, it is reasonable and equitable to put something back. At the end of the day, we all know that none of it is going with us, right? So why not put something back. It seems fair.

time £200,000 a week. Having got into it, trying to rescue it, recognizing that it wasn't possible without the support of the shareholders, who weren't prepared to put any money in it . . . I discovered there were creditors, many of whom were employees, there was no way we could pull out . . . so we are still paying it off. The bill is a big one, for me personally it's in the millions.

Like Owen Oyston, Peter de Savary associates 'giving' to charity with guilt because of the maldistribution of wealth. But in de Savary's case it might be argued that guilt is secondary, and that people who are highly successful seem also to be oriented to the needs of others.

PHILANTHROPY AND ENTREPRENEURS

A good, but unusual, example of philanthropy in our sample is provided by Godfrey Bradman. In the 1980s, Bradman, former Chairman of Rosehaugh PLC, built a £60 million personal fortune and a company worth just under £650 million, by putting together joint ventures and carrying out property developments which added value to underutilized land.

Bradman has backed a wide range of campaigning organizations, including CLEAR, which campaigned for the removal of lead from petrol and paint and the solder in food containers. He set up the Campaign for Freedom of Information and supported International Year of Shelter for the Homeless. He was for many years chairman of Friends of the Earth; has been personally funding research into a vaccine for Aids, and set up the Aids Policy Unit. He also gave £60,000 personally to fund research into hazardous building materials.

Godfrey Bradman has spent millions fighting social 'wrongs' in Britain and abroad, even arranging for high-speed boats to pick up Vietnamese boat-people. Bradman's acts of philanthropy are usually anonymous, and it is worth looking at these acts and the history behind them in more depth. Bradman is the archetypal 'Good Samaritan'. The act of underwriting legal costs to the extent of £5 million from his personal fortune, to the 500 Opren drug sufferers is a case in point. But equally interesting is his empathy and altruistic behaviour, one aspect of which we can describe as 'helping the tramp in the park'.

Bradman recalls:

The other evening, I was out looking at a house with my wife. Behind the house was a park and I walked back to see just what it was like. It was about eight or nine o'clock in the evening, and there in the park I came across a poor old boy. Although he must have been only in his sixties, he was hardly able to walk and in a terrible state – later, we found he had a hernia the size of a large grapefruit – so I asked him if he had somewhere to go, and he didn't. So I said, 'I'll have to try and get you somewhere tonight and see if we can sort you out.'

I'd quite forgotten that my wife was sitting in the car . . . I've got a black taxi, and my wife was sitting in the back so I said, 'This poor boy here' and I introduced them, and I said, 'We have got to get him somewhere!' Anyway, she sat on the jump seat and I sat with her. Once we shut the door the stench was terrible. I dropped her off at Claridges and I said to my chauffeur 'We will have to find somewhere for him. There are some bed and breakfast places in Victoria .' . . . So we went down there, but we couldn't get him in, because the proprietors didn't want him because he smelled. I gave the proprietor more money to compensate. Then the proprietor said he must leave because of the smell, so there was an altercation, we got him into the bathroom . . . . My chauffeur and I worked till midnight scrubbing this chap in the bath, until we had used up all the hot water in the place. We put some clothes on him which we bought, cut off his hair, cut his toenails, which were so long that he could not get his shoes on.

We kept him there for a day, and then I got a geriatric specialist to have a look at him. Then we put him into the Middlesex Hospital, got his clothes sorted out, then traced him through the DHSS and we found that, quite beyond belief, the social worker I got allocated to him turned out to be a trustee of a small fund set up for his benefit. He was due for an inheritance – amazing! . . . I couldn't believe the satisfaction, it was like a fairy story. He is due to inherit in his terms, with the accrued interest, quite a lot of money, the geriatric specialist says.

Like the Victorian entrepreneurs before him, there is a large religious component which directs Bradman's charitable acts. Early in the interview he had said:

I fervently believe that the essence of the Jewish religion is what is called in Hebrew 'Tzdoka', which is charity. . . . I suppose that I view my origins as being exceptional, in the sense that only a minority of Jewish people for sure can trace their ancestors back to the twelve tribes of Israel.

The interview suggests that Bradman's pro-social behaviour also seems to stem from his mother, who served as his principal model:

she would always fight to make sure that I had whatever we needed as children. She motivated me to some considerable extent into being compassionate . . . that you shouldn't tread on people because they cannot protect themselves, that you should be compassionate and caring.

Support of an altruistic character which stems from a moral parental role model combined with a religious background can be explained by referring to several past studies. London (1970), who conducted interviews with people who had rescued Jews from the Nazis during the Second World War, found that almost all identified strongly with at least one parent who had high moral standards and was altruistic. This theme of identification with a 'moral parent' was echoed in interviews with people who committed themselves to the civil rights cause in the US (Rosenhan, 1970).

Since many religions foster concern for others, we might ask: does Bradman, as a religious person, tend to be especially pro-social? Although the evidence is mixed, our research supports the work of Batson and Gray (1981), who suggest that the nature of a person's beliefs may be relevant: what matters may not be whether people worship frequently, but whether their beliefs make them sensitive to the needs of others.

Sir Mark Weinberg is also well known for his charitable work: 'When I set up Hambro Life, I put 10 per cent of my shares into a charitable trust . . . and I set up my own charitable foundation which concentrates on communication among the disabled.'

Sir Mark continues to dedicate a large portion of his time and wealth to helping the deaf, and was a trustee of the Tate Gallery and chairman of the Financial Development Board of the NSPCC. When he started his latest venture, J. Rothschild Assurance, he again put 10 per cent of his interest into a charitable trust.

For Jeffrey Archer, charitable motivation is not a recent phenomenon brought about by new wealth. As a relatively poor student at Oxford, Archer was in part responsible for raising £1 million for Oxfam by arranging for a special Beatles concert. More recent philanthropic acts include his giving £500,000 to charitable causes in 1987, £100,000 of which has gone to the restoration of Ely Cathedral and £50,000 to the Tate Gallery Foundation.

Tony Berry is reported by others as giving vast sums to charitable causes. On a reflective note, Berry says,

> I suppose if you come from . . . a humble background and you achieve success and wealth beyond your wildest dreams, I think you actually feel that you ought to put something back . . . . You actually feel that you have been privileged . . . that somebody up there likes you.

Again, our interview suggests that Peter de Savary's charitable acts stem partly from his mother's influence, which gave him steadfast support together with a sense of moral obligation. This, combined with his strong work ethic, appears a more important motivation for de Savary than the 'guilt associated with wealth' hypothesis.

Gerald Ronson is committed to many philanthropic enterprises. His Ronson Charitable Foundation dispensed some £3 million to 243 charities in 1988. Although Ronson, after the Guinness Affair, fell from grace for a short period, it didn't prevent him from maintaining his previously high profile in charitable works. He is an entrepreneur who devotes 18 hours of his 80-hour working week to charitable organizations: 'As a Jew, I think that it's part of our culture, part of our upbringing . . . it all comes back to what you take out of life you should put back into life . . . our whole belief structure tells us that.'

The interview suggests that Ronson's altruism, like that of several other respondents interviewed, stems mainly from his parents' and religious teachings, and a strong work ethic, combined with his own internalized norms of behaviour and concern for others' needs. More recently, Ronson was reported by the *Sunday Times* (20 September 1992) to have given $5 million to the Ort Mount Carmel School at Daljat el Carmel, in Israel. Although Ronson is Jewish, the school is for children of the Druze religion. The *Sunday Times* reported that 'Ronson's donation is believed to be the largest ever from the Jewish community to a non-Jewish project.'

Other entrepreneurs see ulterior motives in 'giving'. George Davies is not convinced that 'giving' by entrepreneurs is entirely altruistic. Although he gives to charity himself, he sees these acts by others as trying to secure knighthoods for themselves:

> Why, if these guys have so much surplus, don't they give it to their workers? Why go outside the company? . . . It could be because they want a knighthood . . . to give away what you can afford is not really difficult. The question is, why don't they do it in their own businesses? Why don't they create better conditions? It's all very well giving to charity, y'know. Giving money away to the poor and starving and paying your workers a pittance is not consistent.

Teresa Gorman, MP, would certainly agree. She is not very impressed with some philanthropists, whom she sees as status seekers. When asked about charitable acts she argued that:

> People want to be socially accepted. Once that they have made their pile, the next thing they want to have is status. Many of them will give money to a political party in the hope of getting a knighthood or peerage or whatever. In the past it was done openly. Lloyd George was well known for it. And it still goes on. I can name you dozens. You can't eat money. Sometimes you make a trust and do good works. That's perfectly acceptable. Marcus Fox who was then chairman of the candidates list (for the Tory Party) said to me 'Stars and millionaires are ten-a-penny

because once they have done that, the next thing they want to do is to become an MP because it gives them kudos, or status', so it's not the least bit surprising to me.

PHILANTHROPY AND INTRAPRENEURS

The intrapreneurs' approach to giving appears to be different. In general, this group is less impulsive. We recorded only one case where an *individual* received help from an intrapreneur. Here we find that almost all the firms have departments which handle charitable causes in an organized and businesslike manner. Many of the family firms can be seen as susbscribing to acts of social philanthropy. For example, one intrapreneur is attempting to solve the housing problems of the underprivileged blacks in New York: 'I'm getting deeply involved with the key psychological problem of our time, which is how to bring that bottom 10 or 15 per cent of society into the mainstream of American life. Here he is referring to his charitable work in the Harlem ghettos.

Francis Bailey seems to show extreme empathy and a desire for reciprocity

> Well the world has been good to me, for instance in the two schools that I attended. For a long time I didn't have any money to give them but now I've started to give to both schools. They gave to me, so I want to make sure that they remain there – perhaps to help some other young man who comes along. But you must be careful . . . but how can you turn away a hungry child? What you must say to yourself is: how much of the money that you give goes to that hungry child? I try to be careful and understanding.

Martin Laing explains his reasons for 'giving': 'With us it was a religious background. Historically, we had a Christian upbringing so it's quite normal to give some away. We give to organizations with which we have a particular empathy.' Laing, in fact, gives large sums to establishing training schemes for underprivileged children in the inner cities.

Although an anonymous giver to 'good causes' himself, David Jones questions the motives behind some who give large sums to charity: 'I think some of them do it to get knighthoods . . . they want to show everybody what lovely people they are'. David Jones's acts of charity are focused on individuals, and are anonymous. He is responsible for sending children suffering from cerebral palsy to the Peto Institute in Budapest for conductive therapy. Each case costs Jones around £9,000: 'you are the only other fellow in the world that knows this', he said. 'I send the cheques through a solicitor'.

Like Teresa Gorman, the intrapreneur Emma Nicholson, MP, suggests that there is another side to many philanthropists: 'Business leaders and philanthropists fall into very different categories. They become philanthropists to buy respectability and the ones that shout the most do the least.'

THE REASONS FOR PHILANTHROPY AND PRO-SOCIAL BEHAVIOUR

There are several theories purporting to explain pro-social behaviour. Kets de Vries (1977) and Kelly (1970) would argue that *guilt* is a major component in giving, although we found only three cases where guilt was admitted as a possible motive. Kelly assumes that people construe a core role that gives them a sense of identity within a social environment. When that core role is weakened or dissolved, they develop a feeling of guilt.

Kelly (1970) defines guilt as 'the sense of having lost one's core role structure'. In other words, we feel guilty when we behave in ways inconsistent with our sense of who we are. People who have never developed a core role do not feel guilty: they may be anxious or confused, but without a sense of personal identity they do not experience guilt. For example, people without a conscience have no integral sense of self, no core role structure. Such people, Kelly argues, have no stable guidelines to violate and hence will not feel guilty, regardless of their behaviour.

On the other hand, there is considerable support among social psychologists for the 'Good Samaritan' theory of empathy and altruistic motivation (London, 1970; Rosenhan, 1970). This hypothesis seems our 'best fit', as it generalizes to all but six of our respondents.

The normative explanations of helping behaviour suggest that we help others because we have internalized norms, or societal standards of behaviour, and are motivated to act in accordance with those norms. These feelings of obligation motivate us to help, and we are then rewarded by the recognition that we have acted according to our moral standards. Eisenberg-Berg (1979) and Erkut, Jacquette and Staub (1981) argue along similar lines when they write about mature and complex levels of moral judgement, which reflect a concern with broad principles of human rights rather than with self-interest. These levels are associated with a greater willingness to help, which also appears to be related to one's competence and confidence in a particular situation.

Batson and Coke (1981) suggest that there is an important distinction between empathically focusing on another person's distress and being motivated to reduce it, or being concerned with reducing one's own discomfort that has been brought on by the observation of another's distress. Empathic concern may provide a genuinely altruistic motivation for helping. Escaping from the situation, for many people, is an easier and quicker way of reducing one's own unpleasant distress than is helping. By contrast, those experiencing empathic concern continue to help, even when they could easily escape. Thus, empathy, but not personal distress, appears to arouse a genuinely altruistic motivation for helping, which can be satisfied only by seeing another person's suffering end.

However, McClelland (1967) suggests that long-range planning is an integral part of the entrepreneur's personality traits. If this is true, then it might be argued that once the entrepreneur has succeeded on earth, with typical entrepreneurial forethought, he/she might begin looking to secure 'a place in heaven'. One method might be through charitable or philanthropic acts. In Pascalian terms, doing good deeds on earth and believing in God is probably a good wager. Pascal offered a philosophical argument which suggested that a belief in God was one's best bet, as not believing in God would have very negative consequences if God did indeed exist, and would have no consequences if He did not exist; believing in God would have no consequences if He did not exist, but very positive consequences if He did.

HOW DID OUR INTERVIEWEES VIEW CHARITABLE ACTS?

Sir Antony Pilkington has his own special theory about 'giving':

> I have a theory that [giving] relates to our life cycle. I believe that as

---

Harold Woolf on why entrepreneurs give to charity:

If you make say £10 million, well, if you make £100 million or £1,000 million, it's not going to make any bloody difference to the way you eat, the way you dress. You can only drive one car . . . so after a period of time, people get to think, what am I to do with all this money? And so they will buy art maybe, to please themselves, but that will eventually lead them to say: what am I going to do with all this stuff, I'll have to leave it to a museum. So to me it's logical if a man is successful, he will look around and see a wrong and want to right it, and want to do it himself, because he can probably do it better or put his funds to work better. So I think that the small stimulus that Thatcher began to make in people's minds was to think in the way that Victorians used to think, in terms of philanthropy and charity. I think that people will use their own money a hell of a damn sight better than the government.

people grow older, most of them lose the ambition to make money . . . they begin to shed all the paraphernalia of wealth: the extra house, the car, the aeroplane, etc. It all becomes too much hassle. So they begin to distribute their wealth to other people and if they haven't got a large family . . . who else do they pass it on to but charity? After all, if you can completely change a project from failure to success by giving money or some help, that's good and satisfying.

Although we do not have a consensus on why people give to charity, an interesting view of 'giving' is offered by an American intrapreneur. He argues that Jews' and Christians' notion of charity is different. Christians appeal to other Christians' sense of love, whereas Jews approach other Jews for charity because of a sense of one's debt to the other. He identifies three charitable attitudes prevalent among the rich of the US:

1 '*Self-made people* tend on average to be more generous: because they know where it *came from, they can make it again*.
2 The *old rich* who have inherited wealth are more reticent in giving because they feel that it's a wasting asset, or . . . when they give it away, there is no more to replenish it.
3 The last group is the *nouveau pauvre*, the saddest group . . . who have titles, the sense of responsibility, the sense of noblesse oblige . . . . There are the 'Boston Brahmins', heirs of the nineteenth-century fortunes who have run out of money; however, they still have a sense of obligation and feel obliged to subscribe to charitable institutions.

He goes on to say about this last group,

Back in the days when a title of nobility presumably also meant that one followed a noble code, two interesting concepts were taught the young: 'noblesse oblige' and 'obedience to the unenforceable'. The first meant that since you had greater advantages, more was expected of you; the second, that there were some things in life that were 'done' and others that were 'not done'. In such a context, 'rights' implied 'duties', 'privileges' implied 'responsibilities'. By and large these concepts are reasonable guides for today.

However, status-seeking aside, there are 'Good Samaritans' and regardless of the reasons behind 'giving', there is little doubt from the interviews with Bradman, Archer, Jones, Oyston, Berry, Weinberg, Cadbury, Laing and Schroder, that like the Good Samaritan in the Bible, many are given to acts of altruism. They devote a considerable portion of their lives and wealth to 'good works', appearing to seek little earthly reward for their efforts. In the main, they wish to have this portion of their lives remain fairly anonymous.

One of the interesting differences between historical entrepreneurs and the entrepreneurs in our study concerns their lifestyle. George Cadbury, William Hesketh Lever and Jesse Boot all lived frugal lives; Lever even went to the extreme of building an unheated glass structure on the roof of his house which he used as a bedroom, summer and winter, for the major part of his life. This is not the case with business leaders in our study. All seem to have an extremely affluent lifestyle, enjoying fully the material fruits of their labours.

EXECUTIVE SUMMARY

- Both groups, entrepreneurs and intrapreneurs, were in large part charitable, engaging in different ways in acts of 'giving' and philanthropy.
- Regardless of the stereotyped media image of entrepreneurs, as hardnosed and greedy businessmen and women, there were many acts of pro-social behaviour, and some respondents seemed to be simply 'Good Samaritans'. Generally, their acts of philanthropy or charity were anonymous, and we needed to ask leading questions before they would divulge them.
- In some cases, guilt seems to have been the main motivator for acts of charity. Others saw a chance to promote their firms by being associated with 'good works', and some glimpsed the possibility of knighthoods or other honours which might accrue from such acts.
- Basically, the self-reports from our interviewees suggest that charitable acts stem mainly from their parents' and religious teachings of moral obligation, together with a strong work ethic, combined with internalized norms of behaviour and concern for others' needs.

9 The elite business leader

Having spent hundreds of hours interviewing elite business leaders, we shall here draw together the information we have discovered which we feel contributes to being a successful elite entrepreneur or intrapreneur. The group of highly successful entrepreneurs who form the basis of this study seem to possess a number of personal characteristics in common that appear to be related to their success. While it might be possible to operate successfully at the top without all of these attributes, it clearly makes success less risky if they are present. Obviously not all entrepreneurs had all the characteristics, and it may be that one method used to enable the entrepreneur to succeed was to surround him/herself with a top team of executives with compensating abilities. This, according to Cox and Cooper (1988), makes it all the more important to understand which characteristics are important, and which of these one does or does not possess. Some key characteristics which we found will now be considered.

ASSERTIVENESS

Successful entrepreneurs and intrapreneurs were both determined and assertive characters. This trait came through clearly during the interviews. *Determination* may well be a characteristic derived from their early experiences, which for many involved situations (e.g. separation from their parents in childhood, or some form of scapegoating and marginalization in their youth) which required them to take responsibility themselves. Bradman, Berry, Nicholson, Weinberg and Broackes are typical examples. In Bradman's case he had to care for his mother at a relatively tender age in his development, after his father had left. Entrepreneurs needed determination to survive, and survive they did. This survival instinct, if favourably rewarded, may have triggered a response that set a pattern for later life.

THE LEARNING CURVE

Most entrepreneurs, and to a lesser degree intrapreneurs, had experienced setbacks during their careers, but had taken advantage of these 'opportunities' for learning and development. Some had suffered catastrophic financial failure (Archer, Young, Shah, Davies and Jones), others had 'burdened' themselves with what appeared to be loss-making firms (David Alliance and David Jones), only to turn them round into profitable enterprises. Still others, like Leonard van Geest, were 'thrown in at the deep end'. The common characteristic of the entrepreneur and intrapreneur alike is that they survived, coped with the situation, and learned a great deal in the process. This characteristic probably also derives from their early experiences and is akin to determination.

AMBITION

All interviewees in this study were highly proactive and responded to challenge. Most intrapreneurs had been offered high levels of responsibility at a relatively early age and had grasped the opportunity with enthusiasm. Often the challenges were quite daunting, but we never hear of them shrinking from these: once committed, they become dedicated to the problem at hand.

Entrepreneurs, on the other hand, having stooped to conquer the marketplace, are familiar with the very material substance of their enterprise; as Gilder (1986, p. 247) describes it 'the very grit and grease of their businesses'.

Owen Oyston on learning from failure:

There is a learning curve in life and you have to go through certain experiences, I believe, experiences which are not successful, experiences which will help you to have a more rounded view of life and without those experiences, without that build-up of your memory bank, I don't believe that you really do achieve that success. If it comes early in life, very often it isn't sustained. But if you have been through the crises of businesses and you have had failures and you have had this fear that you would never amount to anything, that drives you on, that gives you the spur.

ACHIEVEMENT ORIENTATION

All interviewees were ambitious individuals with a high need to achieve. Many measure their success by satisfying that inner sense of achievement. Entrepreneurs more so than intrapreneurs seem to be motivated by a belief that they could succeed. However, a significant number of entrepreneurs felt a tangible 'fear of failure' in their operation.

'THE INTERNAL GYROSCOPE'

Part of the entrepreneurs' positive approach to life was due to their high level of self-confidence, which in turn reflects clear 'internal reference-points', used to guide their actions. They had a clear view of how they were going to operate in the world. In Chapter 7 we saw that this same trait also applied to intrapreneurs, but to a lesser degree. As Lord Young suggests, the entrepreneur should be capable of succeeding within the existing framework of society. Ideally the entrepreneur has high energy and is a productive member of society. His/her talents are used to contribute, not manipulate.

Sir Antony Pilkington on values:

Question: Several studies have shown entrepreneurs as being motivated mainly by power, wealth, independence or the need to achieve. How would you rank these traits?

Answer: I'm not sure that I would rank any of them personally. I think people believe that they have more power or independence than they really have. I believe they confuse position with power. Inherited wealth is luck. I've always had a reasonable amount of money, I've always had enough to live a comfortable life. I never wanted to be considerably richer, I'm quite happy as I am. Achievement? Well yes, you let yourself down if you don't achieve. There is no satisfaction doing a job such as the chairman of a large public company if you don't believe you are actually achieving something. You want some little place in history. You may not have run the country, but at least you ran a good company, were a good chairman, and the business prospered under you.

INTEGRATED VALUE SYSTEM

Most interviewees had a clear set of values, well articulated in our interviews. One key value displayed by both intrapreneurs and entrepreneurs was *integrity*, which implies being dependable: Davies, Peter de Savary and Laing are excellent examples. When asked to rank *wealth, power, independence* and the *need to achieve*, wealth and power came low on both groups' ranking. Emphasis was also placed on *people and relationships*, which was felt to be important for individuals whose success is measured in organizational terms.

EFFECTIVE MANAGEMENT OF RISK

Intrapreneurs were not high risk-takers. Sir John White of Hanson PLC, it is reported, and Sir Antony Pilkington, see themselves as risk-averse and take every possible step to eliminate risk before they enter into an acquisition or field a new product. Entrepreneurs, as we have seen, are greater risk-takers. But later in their careers, as responsibility burdens the entrepreneurs and they have more to lose, they become more 'calculated' risk-takers.

GOALS: 'DO-ABLE' LISTS OR 'WISH-LISTS'

Entrepreneurs start by breaking the settled mould and creating for themselves, 'do-able' lists of goals as opposed to 'wish-lists'. 'Do-able' goals are ideas based on sound economic reasoning. In typical entrepreneurial style, Peter de Savary, when asked about these lists replied: 'If I wish *something*, I generally go out and *do* it.'

George Davies on integrity:

I like to think I am respected because of my integrity. There's very little integrity about. Integrity means that if I say I'll do something, I'll never let anybody down. I won't wheedle out of it if it turns bad on me. People know me as tough but they know I would never say, 'No, I didn't say that to you.' I don't mind saying to somebody, 'I hired you, I made the bloody cock-up, it has not worked out, but seeing that I've made the cock-up let's try and sort it out instead of having a battle every day.'

Leonard van Geest on risk:

Propensity to risk changes over time . . . but strangely enough, at say 18 years of age and now, I would probably place myself in about the same place but for a totally different set of reasons. As an 18-year-old there was a fair degree of sheer greenness and belief in oneself. I have gone through phases where one says to oneself, 'Let's play it a little safer now,' to the point now where I have a different confidence. Obviously I'm not so green . . . I wouldn't take a flyer. Now being a PLC, does change things from being a family company. I suspect that as you get older you also become more aware of those around you, whether they be stockholders in the company or your own family. I think that, as a young man, it's to do with a very hungry greenness in you. You actually believe that you can turn the world upside-down – you don't see the risk to the same degree.

Intrapreneurs universally stressed the need to be clear about the long-term objectives of their enterprise, probably because many firms were family organizations, with the intrapreneurs seeing their role as that of a 'steward'.

Both intrapreneurs and entrepreneurs understand that a progression of steps is required to achieve real-world goals. To implement their plan, business leaders must be able to communicate and have the cooperation of the other implementors of the plan.

HIGH DEDICATION TO THE JOB

Both entrepreneurs and intrapreneurs in this study worked extremely long hours and regarded their firm as by far the most important element of their lives, with the possible exception of their families. Clearly, much of their personal fulfilment and confirmation of their worth as successful individuals came from their dedication to the work ethic.

INTRINSIC MOTIVATION

This can be seen as a corollary of both groups' dedication to their enterprises. If work is not intrinsically motivating, one can't be dedicated to it. All entrepreneurs in this study are steeped in the work ethic and found their jobs most enjoyable; intrapreneurs to a lesser degree. One of the strongest

David Jones on single-mindedness:

I came here and decided that one of my ambitions in life was to create a successful environment in which people were actually going to be happy working.

Having got that as a general theme I then said: Grattan was an unsuccessful company, how am I going to make it successful? It was then that I started to become an entrepreneur and look for new avenues and developments. What was the question again? [Are entrepreneurs different from other people?]. Yes, absolutely different, in many ways. For instance I don't believe that there is a minute in any day but that you are going to go on, and on and on. Sometimes it's a treadmill and sometimes you have problems because you can get too complacent and you begin to think that everything you do turns to gold. If you have the odd problem or crisis you concentrate your mind on solving that crisis, before you move on to the next one.

You have to be single-minded in what you want to achieve. Your home life will inevitably suffer if you haven't got the right partner, because you neglect your kids, you neglect the family – your job dominates your life. With most ordinary people, their home dominates their life and the job is just a means of making money to go to the pub and buy their fags and take a holiday every six months. You are definitely apart.

impressions we gained from both groups concerned the universal *energy* engendered by the work itself.

WELL-ORGANIZED LIFESTYLE

There was little evidence of serious conflict between work and home life in either group. This was mainly due to the unshakeable support of the spouse, and how well both lives were organized in a realistic and acceptable time frame. In several cases, we found 'entrepreneurial duos', with the wife taking an active part in the development of the enterprise. As evidence, we turn to the wives of Owen Oyston and Sir Mark Weinberg: both are instrumental in the operation of the enterprise and, in fact, are entrepreneurs in their own right.

PRAGMATIC APPROACH

The approach to life of the successful elite entrepreneur is essentially pragmatic, not intellectual. This is evident in spare-time activities, which were on the whole very practical. Few entrepreneurs mentioned intellectual interests or pursuits. In contrast, several intrapreneurs did follow intellectual pursuits, and in some cases academic involvement.

SOUND ANALYTIC AND PROBLEM-SOLVING SKILLS

Entrepreneurs emphasize the importance of being able to analyse a problem and reach an effective solution quickly. This was seen as a fundamental skill. Both Eddy Shah and Tony Berry said that their managers sometimes struggle for hours over problems to which they can see the solutions almost immediately. This is not seen as a highly intellectual exercise by either Berry or Shah, but as the ability to recognize the root cause of a problem. Quite often this can be interpreted as 'intuitive' rather than strictly rational: it was referred to by Owen Oyston as having a 'gut feeling'. However, this recognition of 'root causes' might be looked at differently. We recall that in Homan's theory on *Social Status and Stratification* (1968), people of 'high status' like Shah and Oyston are allowed to take greater risks – without loss of status – than middle managers. Put another way, 'The boss can afford to make more mistakes.'

HIGH LEVEL OF 'PEOPLE-SKILLS'

Since all leaders, by definition, achieve their organizational objectives through other people, it follows that, to be successful, they must have a high degree of interpersonal skills. Most entrepreneurs seem to operate an 'open and consultative' style, but with a strong authoritarian back-up. This approach to business management is demonstrated by Davies, Berry and Peter de Savary, who all report running 'tight ships'. Intrapreneurs are less authoritarian. However, regardless of the style, which can range from authoritarian to participative, the skills required are the same. These include the ability to select appropriate team members, communication skills, and the maintenance of motivation.

HIGH LEVEL OF INNOVATION

All entrepreneurs who completed the Kirton Adaptation/Innovation Inventory were in the upper half of the distribution, that is, they were 'innovators' rather than 'adaptors'. They were the sort of people who, in making changes, would not be constrained by the existing system, but would challenge existing procedures and assumptions, thus producing something 'new' rather than modifying what currently exists. This is an important characteristic for someone who is responsible for the long-term development of a large organization. Intrapreneurs were, in relative terms, less innovative than entrepreneurs.

PARENTAL INFLUENCE

Both the intrapreneurial managers and independent entrepreneurs had mothers who played dominant roles in their early childhood and career path (Owen Oyston, Sir Mark Weinberg, Godfrey Bradman, George Davies, Francis Bailey and others). A very small number of the entrepreneurs reported poor relations with their fathers during their childhood, which led them to be independent and self-sufficient from an early age; Chris Nicholson is one of the more dramatic cases. After he had become successful, Nicholson set about searching for his natural father, 'to show him how successful I had

---

David Jones on creativity:

I wouldn't say that I have a fantastic number of good ideas. I'm probably nearer the 'not so many good ideas' end. But a higher percentage of my good ideas turn into reality. Secondly, a lot of my good ideas come from solving existing problems. Say, one-third of my good ideas are original, a third are those that solve existing problems today. The last third is feeding off other people's thoughts and comments. We can be sitting around in the pub with some of the 30-odd people that I have around me and I might say to somebody, 'What we ought to do is that!' Then somebody will spark off a comment, then somebody else, another. By the next morning I have turned their comments into an original idea that is infinitely better.

At the end of the day, entrepreneurs have ideas because they think about what they are doing. Now there are an awful lot of people that leave the building at five o'clock, and I don't criticize them, their main interest is watching the snooker on the box or going to watch Bradford City. I went to Bradford City last night, because we sponsor them. I actually had a great idea last night, it was about telephone selling. By ten o'clock this morning one of the computer lads had given me a complete write-up of the system. Later on this afternoon we are setting up a meeting . . . and that's exactly how it happens.

become'. He relives this search in the interview. Finally Nicholson traced his father to a 'sleazy country club in Nottingham', where he was working: 'I was introduced to this guy, who they said was my father, I said, "I'm Chris," and we talked for a few minutes, then I turned around and walked away.' Nicholson's final realization, on meeting his father, was that they had absolutely nothing in common.

But it was clear that, in general, these successful individuals did not look back at their childhoods as depressing and unhappy: quite the reverse. Most of them recorded their childhood as normal and happy.

SOCIAL ORIGINS

We have seen that socio-economic background affects development and behaviour. Elite independent entrepreneurs were found, in the main, to have working-class origins and did not have entrepreneurial parents. In contrast, the intrapreneurs had predominately upper-middle or middle-class backgrounds.

EDUCATION

There was an expected difference between the *types* of education received by entrepreneurs and intrapreneurs. Predictably, individuals such as Baron Bruno Schroder or Sir Antony Pilkington received a good formal education. Individuals from deprived backgrounds had a less formal, and in some cases a more problematic, education. But regardless of the educational path followed, it never prevented the determined individual from achieving his/her own goals. Whereas the intrapreneur might have been content to stay at the top of his/her organization, for the independent entrepreneur it was just another hill to climb in overcoming adversity, another 'psychological pebble' in the shoe.

CAREER DEVELOPMENT PATTERNS

For some, the pattern of successfully overcoming adversity continued beyond childhood. When the respondents were asked about experiences in their careers that had contributed to their development, entrepreneurs nearly all spoke of occasions when they were faced with challenging assignments that required them to cope without outside support. McCall, Lombardo and Morrison (1988, p. 63) described similar events, which they refer to as assignments: 'learning because you have to in order to succeed, and having that learning reinforced by success, made assignments potent teachers'.

Lord Archer on what it takes to become an entrepreneur:

A desire to be your own boss and therefore probably be unable to conform to working for someone else. I haven't worked for anyone since the age of 24. I work for the BBC, but by nature I found that I had to run my own show. I was running my own company by the age of 27 because I couldn't work for anyone else. I think that it is the belief that you can do it better than anyone else. Whether you can or not is another thing altogether because again, nine people out of ten people fail, but if you don't believe that [you are the best] you cannot be an entrepreneur.

Others, we found, fell into positions of challenge and responsibility early in their careers, both by accident and design.

In the case of the elite independent entrepreneurs, it is almost axiomatic that they will have faced challenges and overcome difficulties in building up their businesses. Similar to several studies by Shapero (1975, p. 85), all showed evidence of extreme resilience and the ability to bounce back from catastrophic situations. Ten of the independent entrepreneurs had experienced complete financial failure, sometimes more than once, but had reconstituted their lives and started again, treating the event as a learning experience. Only one of the elite intrapreneurs recalled such events. A large majority (13 of the 19 who responded to this question) had, in fact, been 'born into' successful organizations, their careers as such being far less turbulent as they followed somewhat linear career paths.

WORK HISTORY

Some entrepreneurs began their careers with transitory career concepts. They found that they could not find a suitable job which would offer them the challenge and responsibility they desired. This can be seen as a form of 'career blocking'. Peter de Savary, for example, found it necessary to emigrate to Canada, because he felt he could make no progress in his career in England.

PHILANTHROPY AND PRO-SOCIAL BEHAVIOUR

Charitable acts and acts of philanthropy were entered into almost equally by both groups. The interviews suggest that acts of altruism stem mainly from parents and religious teachings of moral obligation and a strong work ethic, combined with internalized norms of behaviour and the concern for others' needs. Intrapreneurs' approach to 'giving' is different to that of entrepreneurs. In general, this group is less impulsive. Almost all the firms have departments which handle charitable causes in an organized and businesslike manner.

MARGINALIZATION

The study suggests that social marginalization is almost exclusively the province of entrepreneurs. Nine respondents suffered social marginali zation and scapegoating, generally associated with belonging to an out-grou

Shapero comments that it also helps to come from a group of 'displa persons'. However, Shapero also comments that other groups, who h been made to feel dependent, such as women, do not produce their quot entrepreneurs.

EXECUTIVE SUMMARY

Although both groups achieve much the same thing – wealth, status and power – their paths to success, their motivations and their personality characteristics are, on many counts, significantly different.

Entrepreneurs have usually experienced and can cope with catastrophic financial failure. They are able to rebuild their businesses after collapse. Entrepreneurs are far less likely to have had support and help from others (mentors or 'guardian angels') than intrapreneurs. Equally expected is that elite entrepreneurs are greater risk-takers and tend to be 'inner directed'. Intrapreneurs, in the main, being 'other directed', are more risk averse. Entrepreneurs can usually point to some significant shaping event which set them on their present career paths.

However, members of both groups also had several common dimensions. They all work extremely long hours, both groups are steeped in the work ethic, both groups are philanthropists. They are intrinsically motivated by, interested in, and find enjoyment in their work and the sense of achievement it provides.

Although all are multi-millionaires, most claim that wealth was not their main motivator. Wealth can be seen as a by-product of these successful men and women, who do what they enjoy doing. They see themselves as having good 'communication' and 'decision-making' skills. This is not surprising: they are attributes to be expected of successful 'high flyers' (Cox and Cooper, 1988). Both groups have, 'A desire to do well, not so much for the sake of social recognition or prestige, but for the sake of an inner feeling of personal accomplishment' (McClelland, 1967).

It is the differences, however, which are sometimes the most interesting. Successfully coping with extreme difficulties while very young seems to set a pattern of resilience and the ability not merely to cope with but to *learn from adversity*. It is this ability which is, we suspect, the key attribute of these successful individuals. What exactly the mechanism is that sets some people on this course we do not know. It is an area requiring more research.

We have seen that the most significant finding from this study is that many successful entrepreneurs do not learn their skills from formal development programmes, but from 'real life' experiences. This is consistent with much psychological theory, in particular that of Carl Rogers, who in *Freedom to Learn for the 80s* (1983), maintains that learning, to be effective, must be of immediate significance to the learner. Reg Revans, in *Action Learning* (1980), argues that effective learning must involve challenge and risk: 'the future of the individual must in some way be influenced by the learning situation'. This was true of many independent entrepreneurs.

The independent entrepreneurs' ability to overcome failure and setbacks is awesome. According to Lord Young, it is this 'do-able' philosophy that keeps them winning. If success means deciding what you want to do then going out and doing it, perhaps by studying these high-flyers, others may benefit by learning how to achieve their own goals. After all, truly well adjusted individuals, in harmony with the environment and community, do not need to achieve great things but simply their own ambitions.

10 Epilogue – Where now for entrepreneurship?

SHIFTING PERSPECTIVES

Porter and Lawler (1968) argue that, prior to the 1950s, it was part of American folklore that the way to succeed in business was to follow in the footsteps of great individualists like Henry Ford, John D. Rockefeller and Andrew Carnegie. They explained that these were 'self-made men' of single-minded dedication, known for their forcefulness and imagination. They were seldom accused of tact or caution. They were 'inner-directed', independent, self-sacrificing persons – those who generate their own values in life.

With the advent of the 1950s, Porter and Lawler explain, and in particular with the publication of two books – *The Lonely Crowd* by Riesman (1950) and *Organization Man* by Whyte (1956) – these qualities were seriously questioned. The thrust of both books was that the individual no longer had a place in middle and lower middle management in the large corporations. According to Riesman, for example, success was more likely to be achieved by the 'other-directed' (outer-directed) person, the individual who is super-sensitive to the thinking and desires of others, the individual who complies with the norms of a situation and adheres to the values of the organization.

Mageean (1980) argues that, from the Second World War onwards, writers have proclaimed the eclipsing of the entrepreneur by bureaucratic organizations, with their corporate decision-making and risk-bearing. The inner-directed man is being replaced, according to Riesman, by the other-directed man who uses the behaviour and thinking of people around him as guides for his own thinking and behaviour. Inner direction is typical of the 'old entrepreneurs', while other direction is becoming the typical characteristic of the 'new middle class as exemplified by the bureaucrat and the salaried employee in business'.

If what Riesman says is true, how does one get to the top in business today? According to Riesman, to get to the top in large organizations, one has to learn a 'personality-oriented specialty or manipulative skill'. The clear direction of Riesman's argument is that other-directed role perceptions and role behaviour are the qualities required for success in business today, and not the inner-directed role exhibited by many entrepreneurs.

Six years after Riesman's book appeared, William H. Whyte, Jr attacked the business world much more directly in *The Organization Man*. Whyte spoke of the social ethic and of the kind of behaviour it requires of one who is to succeed in the large organizations. Whyte's thesis fits in easily with Riesman's views. According to Whyte, the modern American firm, especially the large firm, demands a type of conformity and a go-along-with-the-crowd behaviour. Managers are pictured by Whyte as being rewarded for being non-controversial, adaptable and, in short, for 'not rocking the boat'. The 'organization man', says Whyte, must sacrifice some of his individuality and creativity if he is to succeed.

Whyte was expressing his concern with a shift he observed in the American middle class, from individualistic to organizational attitudes and behaviour. Bureaucratic or organizational men, unlike the individualistic entrepreneur, are more risk averse and more security conscious, seeking refuge in the organization, which discourages unorthodoxy and creativeness. This aversion to individualistic enterprise, however, was not present among top executives, whom Whyte found to be still motivated essentially by the old individualistic competitive drives.

Cochran (1969) writes: 'it is reasonable to suppose, that a generation of executives was being trained with fewer fixed values, less secure principles, greater tendencies to be influenced by those around them . . . in a word, to be good organization men'. The executive plays a role conditioned by his background, his childhood experiences, the values imparted to him by his parents, and values he has absorbed from the changing society. The similarity between Cochran's, Whyte's and Riesman's arguments is obvious: whether you call him an 'organization man' or 'other-directed' is inconsequential. For these authors, 'the adaptable, socially attuned individual is going to succeed in business, while the creative, independent individual is in for trouble' (Porter and Lawler, 1968).

'ASSOCIATIVE MAN'

Certainly, Toffler (1971), one of the theory builders of the 1960s, even though he recognizes the implications of the tempo of change for economic enterprise and security (Mageean 1980), is not convinced that the 'age of the entrepreneur' is dead. What he sees as happening is a resurgence of entrepreneurism within organizations. With the passing of economic insecurity and the coming of affluence, a new willingness to take risks emerges: 'Men are willing to risk failure because they cannot believe they will ever starve.' This new type of organization man, Toffler argues, gives a transient allegiance to organizations, but only to the extent that the association interests him and helps promote his career. Hence the new term given by Toffler – 'Associative Man'.

Toffler explains this point succinctly:

Where the organization man was immobilized by concern for economic security, Associative Man increasingly takes it for granted. Where the organization man was fearful of risks, Associative Man welcomes it (knowing that in a fast changing society even failure is transient). Where the organization man was hierarchy-conscious, seeking status and prestige within the organization, Associative Man seeks it without . . . . Where the organization man dedicated himself to the solution of routine problems according to well defined rules, avoiding any show of unorthodoxy or creativity, Associative Man, faced by novel problems, is encouraged to innovate.

(Toffler, 1971)

Recalling that Toffler was writing at the end of the 1960s, the obvious question is: if economic insecurity returns, will 'Associative Man' become more cautious? Rubin, a Wall Street entrepreneur interviewed on BBC2, thinks he will. Rubin argues this point when he described the 'yuppies' in 1988, and the stock market crash on Black Monday, 19 October 1987. He feels that some consolidation and caution in the market-place is being observed. Rubin explains the problems experienced by innovators and entrepreneurs over the past 30 years. He saw the 1960s and part of the 1970s as being 'moral confrontation' decades, when hippies and many others thought they had the answer to the rich/poor question: love and flower power. This was unrealistic, he contends, as it took no account of how things actually get done. The 1970s was the 'introspection' decade; the 1980s has been the 'moneymaking' decade.

Recession in the late 1980s and early 1990s has brought about more moral confrontation and more introspection. Manufacturing is being squeezed, service will become the theme of the 1990s and we will all become 'greener'. By service we mean unselfish service, that is, that we can be for ourselves and for others at the same time. In fact, enlightened self-interest requires service to others because of our interdependence.

'ENTERPRISING SELF'

More recently, Paul Heelas, writing on Thatcherism in the 1980s suggests that:

> The long-standing Thatcherite emphasis on institutional [market] reform to effect the rejuvenation of capitalism remains very much in force today. But as the 1980s have progressed, increasing attention has been paid to ensuring that the 'new' world of enterprise is populated by people whose self-understanding and psychological functioning is of the right kind. Arguably, a government intent on reforming attitudes, desires, values, expectations and goals must present a well-articulated, internally coherent, and psychologically plausible model to direct people to the desired end.

(Heelas, 1991)

What this suggests is that Thatcher saw the economic downturn in 1989–90 as transient, and that no redirection was necessary.

One characteristic developed under Thatcherism was the 'enterprising self', which was defined by Norman Fowler at the launch of the Enterprise in Higher Education Initiative. The individual is envisaged as 'generating and taking ideas and putting them to work; taking decisions and taking responsibility; taking considered risks; welcoming change and helping to shape it; and creating wealth. . . . [All should acquire] key managerial and business competencies' (*Times Higher Education Supplement*, 1 July 1988).

'YUPPIE MAN'

But the 'Enterprising Self' was not alone in the 1980s. He existed alongside 'yuppie man' who was also a creation of that decade. To many, 'yuppie man' – generally seen as a currency or property dealer – made millions of pounds or dollars without satisfying any social needs. For example the real estate explosion of the 1980s touched off countrywide house building and office construction, but it is doubtful if all that building has made the cities any more beautiful. Simply, the 1980s was a money-making decade. There were notable exceptions. Bradman's Broadgate property developments, which represented Britain's corner in the New York/Tokyo/London stock market Golden Triangle, was one. Again, many of Bradman's projects added value to under-utilized land and one interesting venture was his proposal for a 'self-build housing initiative' to aid the disadvantaged and unemployed in the inner cities. This was planned to be the biggest house-building programme Britain had ever seen.

The over-exuberance of the 1980s caused the pendulum of change to swing too far, and it was considered by many to be the most selfish of decades. The second Wall Street crash on 'Black Monday', 19 October 1987, was the correction for the financial expansion of this period. A correction also for the yuppies, who found their Porsches disappearing with the housing and currency market; it forced everyone to put money into perspective. In the 1990s we saw runs on sterling, the franc and the peseta as the foreign currency departments of the great banks and independent currency dealers drove currencies into devaluation and governments into turmoil. All this did little to help the group which might be called the 'ordinary man'. 'Black Wednesday' – 16 September 1992 – is seen as a corrective to this swing and seems to suggest that re-adjustment and consolidation are still taking place in the market.

Just as moneymaking was the passion of the 1980s, so changing society will be the passion of the 1990s. We see a need to create products that will not pollute the world, and that will be the answer to human needs. In the 1980s the equalitarians of the 1960s became elitists who respected people who knew how to get things done. Maybe we have concluded that meritocracy was necessary. Perhaps people should be rewarded differently for different achievements. None of us has the answer; we are still learning about business and money – we are in school, but we have no teachers. We must become our own teachers, making it up as we go along, we are per-petual pioneers. Whilst we are not yet in a position to chart the course of entrepreneurship in the 1990s, the examples of 'Economic', 'Self-actualizing', 'Organization', 'Associative', 'Enterprising Self' and 'Yuppie Man' will serve to illustrate what we might call the 'motivations' of entrepreneurial activity.

Finally, it is interesting to hypothesize that what we are observing may not be some random hiccup in the market or the cyclical recurrence of peaks and troughs, but a desire by many to slow down change. It is interesting to note that the observations of societies at different times and different places show that substantial restraints upon entrepreneurial activ-ity are commonplace. The presence of these restraints suggests that there is a desire for continuity in most societies, an upper limit on the rate of innovation more than which society will not tolerate. What we can ask is, 'Did we reach some sort of entrepreneurial saturation in the 1980s?'

WHERE ARE THEY NOW?

Our sample was drawn in part from 'Britain's Richest 200 People' (*Money Magazine*, March 1988), and 'The Thatcher Revolution' (*Sunday Times*, May 1987). The *Sunday Times* has published a supplement called 'Britain's

Rich: The Top 300' (May 1992), and it is interesting to see how some of the more prominent members of our sample rate in the most recent league table of wealth, in comparison with that of five years previously.

What is immediately noticeable in 'Britain's Rich: the Top 300' is the stability of old established family firms. Even during a prolonged recession they are well represented, with pride of place going to oldest money – our research added support to the *Sunday Times* report. Of the 46 respondents interviewed for this work, 13 had inherited substantial money, and they can still be seen maintaining their wealth through both the boom and bust years. A few typical examples are Sir Adrian Cadbury, Sir Antony Pilkington, Sir Kenneth Kleinwort, the late Lord McAlpine of Moffat, Julian Smith, Norman Burrough and Sam Whitbread. It is true that many have suffered setbacks, but all have weathered the recession with only minor bruising.

Equally noticeable is the fallout suffered amongst the entrepreneurs who made their fortunes in the property boom of the 1980s. One of the seminal figures of the 1980s property scene, in which some of his schemes reshaped the commercial face of London, was Godfrey Bradman, the philanthropist and property developer. His moving on from Rosehaugh PLC is directly related to the crash in commercial office property values brought about by the recession. Bradman no longer rates a position as one of the richest 300.

Tony Berry, the entrepreneur behind one of Britain's biggest successful financial take-over bids, when he secured Manpower Inc., the largest employment agency in the world, fell from grace when insider share dealings by others and an unsecured loan was discovered. He resigned from the board and currently operates Technologies PLC, a city firm. He is still a director of Tottenham Hotspur Football Club, but also no longer features in Britain's richest 300.

Nor is Peter de Savary, entrepreneurial property developer, once owner of the northernmost and southernmost tips of Britain any longer among Britain's 300 richest people. Recession in the property market has caused Participates PLC, to retrench.

Gerald Ronson, when interviewed for this research, was the fifteenth-richest man in Britain. After his part in the Guinness affair and the effects of the recession Ronson is no longer one of Britain's richest 300.

George Davies, removed as managing director of NEXT PLC, the firm he had created, has surfaced again under the name of Davies Associates PLC. He is currently heavily involved with ASDA, the supermarket chain. Davies has twice been brought down, once by secondary banks calling in loans, and most recently in a boardroom battle with David Jones (another of our interviewees), which he lost.

But few should worry for Davies: he will return, he is the archetypal survivor, the true innovative entrepreneur.

Not all entrepreneurs in our sample suffered or were brought down during the recession. Victor Kiam, the American entrepreneur, has, through hard work, continued to go from strength to strength.

Harold Woolf, the entrepreneurial London chemist and adherent of the Russian economist, Nikolai Kondratieff (who identified cycles of economic activity), allowed us to be a 'fly on his wall' during the period 1987–93, and we can follow his entrepreneurial activities – selling out his chain of chemists to Boots the Chemist, searching out new ventures and acting as a 'guardian angel' to his son.

1987 Several trips to the Soviet Union to establish potential there for Underwoods [his chain of chemists].

1988 More of the same. However, in November Boots came up with an offer, not to be refused, which was signed a few days later. This was quite good timing as (a) I thought we were going into severe recession, comparable to the 1930s, and (b) I thought that interest rates were going to go up. Any regrets? Yes, I suppose it's like a divorce. Your former love is married to someone else and you are alone. But overall I'm pleased with the sale.

1990 Travel, investments, looking for opportunities, but with *patience*, more *patience*, and yet more *patience*.

1991 Eldest son qualified as a chartered accountant. Did not want to continue in the profession. Thought the UK was going into recession and said, 'What about the East, Dad?' So we both went to Berlin, Budapest, Vienna and Prague to look for opportunities. He stayed in Prague, I visited.

1992 Retail, property and publishing business started in Prague. Son married to a young, attractive workaholic. I continue to visit and advise.

1993 Joined board of Czech company and now working permanently in Prague with son and wife. Ten shops selling t-shirts, modern glass and a book, *Art and History of Prague*, in several languages with sales of over 140,000 p.a. at circa £10 each.

Bought several buildings comprising some 150 flats, offices and shops, slowly being converted and refurbished for lease to Western companies. A real success story for a young man and his wife in a new country, not speaking the language and with little experience. Company employs about 100 people.

Woolf could have continued to 'safely' operate his chain of chemists as he had done for years. He could have substituted his natural entrepreneurial dynamism for security. However, Woolf knows that the greatest risk of all is not to take risks.

Entrepreneurs have long been dubbed 'shooting stars', and in some respects this analogy is accurate: many are indeed high-flyers and some of the fragile structures they create do burn out when continually exposed to the atmosphere of a market in recession. But there the analogy ends. Entrepreneurs have the ability to start afresh, and generally they do.

The demise of many 1980s 'shooting stars' has reinforced another feature of our sample. It appears that you can't beat the greater stability of old family wealth. When Sir Antony Pilkington was questioned about the meteoric rise of Richard Branson his reply was: 'Come back in 50 years and I'll tell you if he was a success or not.'

Another interesting feature emerging from the research – which should be an object lesson to any budding entrepreneurs, is that many of the 1980s figures who are still around today are those who sold out, those who moved on to another challenge, those who did not linger too long. Owen Oyston sold his estate agency business the Thursday before the stock market crash of October 1987. Sir Mark Weinberg sold out through a nagging fear of catastrophic failure. Edward Jackson sold out just before the property crash in 1987. Perhaps what we need to discover is when to sell!

References

Asch, S.E. (1953) *Social Psychology*, cited in Homans, G.C. (1968) *Social Behaviour, its Elementary Forms*, Routledge & Kegan Paul, London.

Batson, C.D. and Coke, J.S. (1984) 'Empathy: a source of altruistic motivation for helping?', in Deaux, K. and Wrightman, L.S. (eds) *Social Psychology in the 80s*, Brooks/Cole Publishing Co., Monterey.

Batson, C.D. and Gray, R.A. (1981) 'Religious orientation and helping behaviour: responding to one's own or the victim's needs?', *Journal of Personality and Social Psychology* 40: 511–20.

Becker, H.S. (1958) 'Problems of inference and proof in participant observation', *American Sociological Review* 23, December: 652–60.

Bennis, W. and Nauus, B. (1985) *Leaders: The Strategies for Taking Charge*, Harper & Row, New York.

Birch, D.L. (1981) 'Who Creates Jobs?', *The Public Interest* 65.

Blau, P.M. (1955) *The Dynamics of Bureaucracy*, University of Chicago Press, Chicago.

Bouchard, T. (1976) 'All About Twins', *Newsweek Magazine*, 23 November: 69.

Bradley, I.C. (1987) *Enlightened Entrepreneurs*, Bath Press, Avon.

Bruce, R. (1976) *The Entrepreneurs*, Libertarian Books, Folium Press Ltd, Birmingham.

Child, I.L. (1968) 'Personality in Culture', in Borgatta, E.F. and Lambert, W.W. (eds) *Handbook of Personality Theory and Research, Rand McNally, Chicago*.

Clements, R.V. (1958) *Managers: A Study of their Careers in Industry*, Allen & Unwin, London.

Cochran, T.C. (1969) 'Entrepreneurship', *Encyclopedia of Social Sciences:* 87–90.

Collins, O.F., Moore, D.G. and Unwalla, D.B. (1964) *The Enterprising Man*, Bureau of Business and Economic Research, Graduate School of Business Administration, Michigan State University, East Lansing.

Cooper, C.L. and Hingley, P. (1985) *The Change Makers*, Harper & Row, London.

Cox, C. and Cooper, C.L. (1988) *High Flyers: An Anatomy of Managerial Success*, Basil Blackwell, Oxford.

Devereaux, E.C. (1969) 'Child-rearing in England and the United States: a cross sectional comparison', *Journal of Marriage and Family*: 34–57.

Drucker, P.F. (1986) *Innovation and Entrepreneurship*, Pan Books, London.

Drucker, P.F. (1989) *The New Realities*, Mandrin Paperback, London.

Eisenberg-Berg, N. (1979) 'Relationship of prosocial moral reasoning to altruism, political liberalism, and intelligence', *Developmental Psychology* 15: 87–9.

Erkut, S., Jaquette, D.S. and Staub, E. (1981) 'Moral judgement situation interaction as a basis of predicting prosocial behaviour', *Journal of Personality* 49: 1–14.

Eysenck, H.J. and Eysenck, H.B.J. (1963) *The Eysenck Personality Inventory*, University of London Press, London.

Franklin, B. (1736) 'Necessary Hints To Those That Would Be Rich' and 'Advice to a Young Tradesman' (1748), quoted in Weber, M. (1958) (trans. T. Parson), *The Protestant Ethic and the Spirit of Capitalism*, Charles Scribner & Son, New York.

Freud, S. (1949) *An Outline of Psycho-analysis*, Hogarth Press, London.

Gilder, G. (1986) *The Spirit of Enterprise*, Penguin Books, Harmondsworth.

Griffiths, B. (1982) *Morality and the Market Place: Christian Alternative to Capitalism and Socialism* (2nd edn), Hodder & Stoughton, London.

Hall, D.T. (1976) *Careers in organizations*, Goodyear, Santa Monica, CA.

Handy, C.B. (1976) *Understanding Organizations*, Penguin, Harmondsworth.

Heelas, P. (1991) 'Reforming the self: enterprise and the character of Thatcherism', in Keats, R. and Abercrombie, N. (eds) *Enterprise Culture*, Routledge, London.

Hertz, L. (1987) *The Business Amazons*, Methuen, London.

Homans, G.C. (1968) *Social Behaviour: its Elementary Forms*, Routledge & Kegan Paul, London.

Hornaday, J.A. and Bunker, C.S. (1970) 'The Nature of the Entrepreneur', *Personnel Psychology* 23, 1: 47–54.

Hughes, E.C. (1946) 'The Knitting of Racial Groups in Industry', *American Sociological Review* 11: 517. Also in Homans, C.G. (1968) *Social Behaviour*, Routledge & Kegan Paul, London.

Kakabadse, A.K. (1983) *The Politics of Management*, Gower Press, London.

Keat, R. and Abercrombie, N. (1991) *Enterprise Culture*, Routledge, London.

Kelly, G.A. (1970) 'A brief introduction to personal construct theory', in Bannister, D. (ed.) *Perspectives in Personal Construct Theory*, Academic Press, London.

Kelly, H.H. and Shapiro, M.M. (1954) 'An experiment on conformity to group norms where conformity is detrimental to group achievement', *American Sociological Review* 19: 667–77. Also in Homans, C.G. (1968) *Social Behaviour*, Routledge & Kegan Paul, London.

Kets de Vries, M.F.R. (1977) 'The entrepreneurial personality: a person at the crossroads', *Journal of Management Studies* 14, 1: 33–57.

Kets de Vries, M.F.R. (1980) 'Stress and the Entrepreneurs', in Cooper, C.L. and Payne, R. (eds) *Current Concerns in Occupational Stress*, Wiley, Chichester.

Kets de Vries, M.F.R. and Miller, D. (1989) *The Neurotic Organization*, Jossey-Bass, London.

Kirton, M.J. (1976) 'Adaptors and innovators: a description and a measure', *Journal of Applied Psychology* 61, 5: 622–9.

Knight, F.H. (1940) *Risk, Uncertainty & Profit* (5th edn), Houghton-Mifflin, Boston.

Komives, J.L. (1972) 'Characteristics of entrepreneurs', *The Business Quarterly* 37, summer: 76–9.

Kotter, J.P. (1982) *The General Managers*, Free Press, New York.

Langer, E. (1980) 'The psychology of chance', in Dowie, J. and Lefrere, P. (eds) *Risk & Chance*, Open University Press, Milton Keynes.

Latane, B. and Darley, J.M. (1976) *Help in a Crisis: Bystander Response to an Emergency*, General Learning Press, Morristown NJ.

Lessem, R. (1987) *Intrapreneurship*, Wildwood House, Aldershot.

Levinson, H. (1971) 'Conflicts that plague family businesses', *Harvard Business Review* March–April: 90–8.

Levy, P. (1974) 'Generalizability studies in clinical settings', *British Journal of Social and Clinical Psychology* 13: 161–72.

London, P. (1970) 'The Rescuers: motivational hypotheses about Christians who save Jews from Nazis', in Macauley, J. and Berkowitz, L. (eds) *Altruism and Helping Behaviour: Social Psychological Studies of Some Antecedents and Consequences*, Academic Press, New York.

Lynn, R. (1986) Personal Communication.

McCall, M.W., Lombardo, M.M. and Morrison, A.M. (1988) *The Lessons of Experience: How Successful Executives Develop on the Job*, Lexington Books, Lexington.

McClelland, D.C. (1967) *The Achieving Society*, Free Press, USA.

McClelland, D.C. (1971) 'The achievement motive in economic growth', in Kilby, P. (ed.) *Entrepreneurship and Economic Development*, Free Press, USA.

Macrae, N. (1976) 'The Coming Entrepreneurial Revolution', *Economist*, December: 41–66.

Mageean, D. (1980) *The World of Monetary Risk*, Open University Press, Milton Keynes.

Margerison, C.J. (1980) 'How Chief Executives Succeed', *Journal of European Industrial Training* 3.

Marshall, J. (1984) 'Women managers: travellers in a male world', Wiley, Chichester.

Mills, C.W. (1956) *The Power Elite*, Oxford University Press, New York.

Morris, P. (1991) 'Freeing the spirit of enterprise: the genesis and development of the concept of enterprise culture', in Keats, R. and Abercrombie, N. (eds), *Enterprise Culture*, Routledge, London.

Mumford, A. (1985) 'What's new in management development?', *Personnel Management*, May: 30–2.

Naisbitt, J. (1984) *Megatrends*, Macdonald, London.

Norburn, D. (1985) *Corporate Leaders in Britain and America: A cross national Analysis*, Working Paper 85.19, Cranfield School of Management, Cranfield.

Pareto, V. (1963) *A Treatise on General Sociology* (ed.) Livingstone, A., Dover, New York.

Pinchot, G. (1985) *Intrapreneuring*, Harper & Row, New York.

Porter, L.W. and Lawler, E.E. (1968) *Managerial Attitudes and Performance*, R.D. Irwin, Illinois.

Revans, R.W. (1980) *Action Learning*, Blonde and Briggs, London.

Riesman, D. (1950) *The Lonely Crowd*, Yale University Press, New Haven.

Rogers, C.K. (1942) *Counseling and Psychotherapy*, Houghton-Mifflin, Boston.

Rogers, C.K. (1983) *Freedom to Learn for the 80s*, Merrill, Columbus.

Rosenhan, D.L. (1970) 'The natural socialization of altruistic autonomy', in Macaulay, J. and Birkowitz, L. (eds), *Altruism and Helping Behaviour: Social Psychological Studies of some Antecedents and Consequences*, Academic Press, New York.

Rotter, J.B. (1966) 'Generalized expectancies for internal versus external control of reinforcement', *Psychological Monographs: General and Applied* 80: 609.

Rotter, J.B. (1971) 'External control and internal control', *Psychology Today*, June: 37–42.

Schumpeter, J.A. (1931) *Theorie der Wirschaftlichen Entwicklung*, Aufl, Munchen und Leibzig: Duncker und Humblat.

Schumpeter, J.A. (1934) *The Theory of Economic Development*, Harvard University Press, Cambridge.

Schwartz, S.H. (1973) 'Normative explanations of helping behaviour: a critique, proposal, and empirical test', *Journal of Experimental Social Psychology* 9: 349–64.

Schwartz, S.H. (1977) 'Normative influences on altruism', in Berkowitz, L. (ed.) *Advances in Experimental Social Psychology* 10, Academic Press, New York.

Schwartz, S.H. and Howard, J.A. (1981) 'A normative and decision-making model of altruism', in Rushton, J.P. and Sorrentino, R.M. (eds) *Altruism and Helping Behaviour: Social, Personality, and Developmental Perspectives*, Erlbaum, Hillsdale.

Seligman, M.E.P. and Maier, S.F. (1967) 'Failure to escape traumatic shock', *Journal of Experimental Psychology*, 74: 1–9.

Shapero, A. (1975) 'The displaced, uncomfortable entrepreneurs', *Psychology Today*, November: 83–5.

Silver, D.A. (1986) *The Entrepreneurial Life*, Wiley, New York.

Sonnenfelt, J. and Koffer, J.P. (1982) 'The maturation of career theory', *Human Relations*, 35: 19–46.

Stanworth, M.J.K. and Curran, J. (1973) *Management Motivation in the Smaller Business*, Gower Press, London.

Tawney, R.H. (1987) *Religion and the Rise of Capitalism*, Peregrine Books, Reading.

Thatcher, D. (1988) Personal Communication.

Toffler, A. (1971) *Future Shock*, Pan, London.

Weber, M. (1958) *The Protestant Ethic and the Spirit of Capitalism*, Charles Scribner & Sons, New York.

White, B. (1989) *A Comparative Study of Female Managers and Female Entrepreneurs*, unpublished MSc Thesis, School of Management, UMIST, Manchester.

White, B., Cox, C. and Cooper, C.L. (1992) *Women's Career Development: High Flyers*, Basil Blackwell, Oxford.

Whyte, W.H. (Jr) (1956) *The Organization Man*, Lowe & Brydone, London.

Index